THE VULTURES · THE WOMAN OF PARIS

THE MERRY-GO-ROUND · BY HENRY BECQUE

THE VULTURES
THE WOMAN OF PARIS
THE MERRY-GO-ROUND

THREE PLAYS BY

HENRY BECQUE

TRANSLATED FROM THE FRENCH
WITH AN INTRODUCTION BY

FREEMAN TILDEN

NEW YORK
MITCHELL KENNERLEY
MCMXIII

THE · PLIMPTON · PRESS
NORWOOD · MASS · U · S · A

CONTENTS

26162

INTRODUCTION

HENRY BECQUE (1837–1899) was one of those men of letters to whom falls the ungrateful lot of giving the public what it does not want. In the very heyday of romanticism, Becque had the effrontery to hawk an entirely different line of wares in the Parisian theatrical markets. He boldly trespassed against the most sacred traditions built up and sustained under the guidance of Sardou. He flouted the "happy ending"; he questioned the infallibility of M. Sarcey; he even thought it possible to write a drama in five acts, when everybody knew that four acts must be the limit. Becque was a revolutionist.

Yet even revolutionists have friends and admirers. Becque had comparatively few, but those few were powerful enough to force the production of plays which, lacking this propulsion of friendship, could never have seen the light. One of these friends was Edouard Thierry, one-time director of the Comédie Française. Another, strange to say, was Sardou — that very Sardou against whose dramatic precepts Becque carried on a merciless warfare.

This man might have been popular. He was Parisian born. He had all the cleverness and knack and sophistication necessary to make him a brilliant transient on the stage of Paris. But he had a big dream, and the dream was to make the stage represent the marvellous dramatic commonplaces of every-day life. He saw that the sentimental nonsense with which the public was being regaled — high-class nonsense though some of it might be — represented a very small corner of Life, if it represented Life at all. The reaction of Becque's mind against the glorification of sentimental impossibilities was terrific. He conceived the idea of a " cruel theatre," in which truth should go defiantly bare; in which the characters should act like human beings instead of wire-worked puppets; in which the action should be the logical course of workday events, without the introduction of spurious material to keep the audience mystified or good-humored. In our day this is an old story. The tide turned against old-school romanticism long ago, and we have our realism so refined that it often has less dramatic action than Life itself. If Becque had fallen into this trap — of being dull — that would have been the end of him. But he happened to be a master of stagecraft; and he knew how to manipulate the surprises of every-day existence, how to reproduce them with telling effect, how to tell a precise story so that the narration would be clear without being obvious. He had also an almost incredible persistence and faith in himself. He was a tireless worker. And he had some good friends. So he was permitted to drive the wedge that opened the way for realism. Becque's followers were many. More than one of them excelled the master in certain details, as was to be expected. They were not pioneering. They had a trail already blazed. It required a brutal strength like Becque's to knock over the idols of romance.

When Henry Becque first came knocking at the stage door, it was with an opera in three acts, " Sardana-pale," an avowed imitation of Lord Byron. With music by Victorin Joncières, a composer of merit, it was presented for the first time at the Théâtre Lyrique early in 1867. It enjoyed some success.

Following the opera came " L'Enfant Prodigue," produced in 1868 at the Vaudeville. The freshness of this piece, with its unconventionality, its deliberately wicked and sometimes savage thrusts, combined with real wit and sprightliness, puzzled the critics a little. The dean of the profession, M. Sarcey, permitted himself to welcome the new dramatic author, and to praise him for his pleasant frivolity. M. Sarcey wrote rather gingerly, however. He evidently wanted to be in a position to beat a quick retreat. " The Prodigal Son " is certainly not great, but as a reading play it is good for the blues. And besides its wit, it contains at least one unexpectedly striking and powerful scene, that of the dinner of the *concierges*. In this scene *Clarisse* sings a curious street-girl song, " Les Pauvr's P'tit's Femmes," of exquisite humanness and pathos.

Following " The Prodigal Son," it was to be expected that Becque, taking advantage of the foothold his vaudeville had given him, should come back with some joyous comedy. He appeared with a five-act drama, " Michel Pauper," a play almost barbarous in its brutality. The wonder now is, not that it was not a success, but that it was ever presented at all. It must have seemed mad as a hatter in 1870. It does, indeed, at this distance, seem to have a touch of madness. It did demonstrate one thing, however: that

Becque could construct a play. He used strange materials, he sounded uncanny depths, but he could write.

After the production of " L'Enlèvement " in 1871 — a mordant comedy of provincial domesticity — Becque had nothing produced until " La Navette," in 1878. This one-act comedy, translated in the present volume under the title " The Merry-Go-Round," is light, malicious, even naughty on the surface. There is much under the surface. Becque's eyes were open in the seventies. He saw a lot of sham.

" Les Honnêtes Femmes," another one-act comedy, was produced in 1880, and then Becque was at last engaged upon more enduring stuff. In the next five years were produced his two finished masterpieces, " Les Corbeaux " and " La Parisienne," and a beginning was made of " Les Polichinelles," unfortunately left undone at the dramatist's death.

" Les Corbeaux " (translated as " The Vultures " in this volume) was produced in 1882 at the Comédie Française. It was by mere chance that it was produced at all. Becque's difficulty was no longer that he was unknown; it was that the theatre-directors knew him only too well. He was a disturber of the peace of mind of quiet folks who wanted to " look on the bright side of things." He was the kind of author that puts out the lights at theatres in mid-season. Becque peddled " Les Corbeaux " from one theatre to another. It was rejected everywhere. Finally there was only one reputable theatre left, and that was the greatest of them all, the Comédie Française. Becque had not even considered the possibility of getting a hearing there. But M. Thierry read the play, and, though it staggered him a little, he recognized the genius in it. He was convinced that it should be put on. He was no longer at the head of the Comédie Française, but a request from him would, of course, be gracefully received by his successor, Émile Perrin. In this least promising of ways, "Les Corbeaux" had its first presentation at the famous theatre on September 14, 1882.

"Les Corbeaux" was not a play calculated to make its author a prime favorite among the run of play-goers. It hurt them. It assailed one of the darling institutions of the country, the notarial system. "You are attacking, offhand, the most respectable body of men I know of; you are bringing under suspicion the law itself," says *Bourdon*, the notary, in the second act of the play, in futile reply to the rude insinuations of the architect *Lefort*. That was just what Becque meant to do! He intended to reveal the possibilities of gross injustice, fraud and graft that lay within the hide-bound, parochial and bureaucratic system which turned out *Bourdons*, and then, even against its will, felt bound to maintain them.

But worse even than his cold-blooded handling of tender subjects in particular, was Becque's general ex-altation of the bourgeois viewpoint. "Exaltation" is a strong word, but it must have been a terrible blow, at a moment when the stage was dedicated to the de-piction of chapters from the lives of the very nicest of people, to find in "Les Corbeaux" that the only representatives of "an old family" were a vicious wo-man, dead broke and fortune-hunting, and her inverte-brate son. Then, besides, Becque's stage settings were held to be too simple. The furnishings had been con-stantly growing more elaborate and expensive, and it seems that the arrangements of Becque might have come as a grateful relief to the theatre directors. It was not so. They did n't like it. It looked cheap.

Becque's social ideas were surprisingly " advanced." He sensed the wrongs of the little people, the underdogs in the struggle for existence. He voiced the protest of women against the prejudice that kept them from earning a decent livelihood and forced them, in one direction, to parasitism, and, in the other direction, to immorality.

Poor *Mrs. Vigneron!* So helplessly naïve and impractical was she that she could imagine herself at the head of her late husband's factory. *Bourdon*, the notary, disillusioned her on that point: " Would it look well for a woman to place herself at the head of a large establishment? "

" La Parisienne," which had its first performance in 1885, was for other reasons a bitter pill to the public. Nobody questioned its wit. It was admitted that the diabolically clever dialogue of the first scene, leading up to the thunderbolt discovery of the audience that *Lafont* is not *Clotilde's* husband, but her lover, was alone worth the price of admission. But the critics, most of them, thought that Becque had slandered the Parisian woman. Someone said that the title of the play should be changed from " La Parisienne " to " Une Parisienne ": but what the temper of the time could not forgive was the ruthlessness with which Henry Becque tore the veil of romance from illicit love — from adultery, if you please — and put it on the prosaic basis of every-day marriage. That was too much. However, as Mr. James Huneker remarks in his delightful essay on Becque, the conventional naughty triangle of the French theatre, after the presentation of " La Parisienne," was done forever.

"La Parisienne" was Becque's last play. At the time of his death he was at work upon "Les Polichinelles," a play even more militant in its social ideas than the others. But though there is reason for regret that Becque's work was cut short, it is certain that with his three volumes of plays he had performed his special mission. It is not too much to say that when Ibsen came upon the field with his great dramas, he had a decided advantage in his struggle from taking possession of the breastworks thrown up and manned by Henry Becque.

A CHRONOLOGICAL LIST OF PLAYS BY HENRY BECQUE

SARDANAPALUS (Sardanapale), 1867;
THE PRODIGAL SON (L'Enfant Prodigue), 1868;
MICHEL PAUPER, 1870;
THE ELOPEMENT (L'Enlèvement), 1871;
THE MERRY-GO-ROUND (La Navette), 1879;
WOMEN OF VIRTUE (Les Honnêtes Femmes), 1880;
THE VULTURES (Les Corbeaux), 1882;
THE WOMAN OF PARIS (La Parisienne), 1885;
THE PUPPETS (Les Polichinelles), unfinished;
THE START (Le Départ);
MADELEINE;
WIDOWED (Veuve);
A FOUR-HANDED GAME (Le Domino à Quatre);
AN EXECUTION (Une Execution).

THE VULTURES

(Les Corbeaux)

A DRAMA IN FOUR ACTS

1882

PERSONS

VIGNERON . . . . *A manufacturer*

TEISSIER

    Formerly a small banker, now Vigneron's partner

BOURDON . . . . *A lawyer*

MERCKENS . . . . *A music-teacher*

LEFORT . . . . *An architect*

DUPUIS . . . . . . *A dealer in house furnishings*

GASTON . . . . *Vigneron's son*

AUGUSTE

A DOCTOR

GEORGE DE SAINT-GENIS

LENORMAND

GENERAL FROMENTIN

MRS. VIGNERON

MRS. DE SAINT-GENIS

MARIE

BLANCHE   *Vigneron's daughters*

JUDITH

ROSALIE

    The action takes place at Paris in our own day.

THE VULTURES

THE FIRST ACT

A luxuriously furnished drawing-room. There are three double doors at the rear, and double doors on the sides. At the right, in the foreground, there is a piano; and at the left, against the wall, a writing-table. Behind this writing-table is a fireplace. At the rear, on the right, a table; at the left, in the foreground, a couch. Other furniture, mirrors, flowers, etc.

When the curtain rises, Vigneron is seen asleep on the couch. He is in a dressing-gown, and has a newspaper in his hands. Marie, seated near him, is engaged in needle-work. Judith is at the piano. Blanche is writing at the table.

MRS. VIGNERON

Don't play any more, Judith; your father is asleep. (*Going over to the table*) Blanche.

BLANCHE

Yes, mama.

MRS. VIGNERON

Is it finished?

BLANCHE

Just one minute.

MRS. VIGNERON

Have you gone over them? How many will there be at table?

BLANCHE

Sixteen.

MRS. VIGNERON

That's good. (*She brings a chair and sits down beside Blanche*)

BLANCHE

Do you think the dinner will be any better for putting a menu at each plate?

MRS. VIGNERON

It won't be any the worse for it, anyhow.

BLANCHE

What a queer custom! But are you quite sure it is the proper thing?

MRS. VIGNERON

Absolutely sure. I saw it in the Ladies' Home Companion.

BLANCHE

Shall we run over the places together?

MRS. VIGNERON

Let's go over the list first. Mrs. Saint-Genis?

BLANCHE

I've got her down.

MRS. VIGNERON

Her son?

BLANCHE

You needn't be afraid of my forgetting him.

MRS. VIGNERON

Father Mouton?

BLANCHE

The dear old man! He baptized me, and confirmed me — and now he is going to marry me.

MRS. VIGNERON

If you are going to gossip about every name we come to, we won't be through by next week. Mr. Teissier?

BLANCHE

I 've got him down. I could get along very well without him, though.

VIGNERON (*waking*)

What 's that I hear? Is Miss Blanche giving orders in my house?

BLANCHE

Goodness, yes, papa; it 's little Blanche.

VIGNERON

And may we know what Mr. Teissier has done to you, miss?

BLANCHE

To me? Nothing. But he is old, and ugly, and boorish, and a miser. And he never looks anybody in the face; that 's reason enough why I don't like him around me.

VIGNERON

Fine! Bully! I 'll fix things all right. Mrs. Vigneron, you need n't save a place at the table for this young lady. She is going to have dinner in her room.

BLANCHE

You 'll be saying soon that the wedding will go ahead without me.

VIGNERON

If you say another word, you shan't be married — Oh! (*A pause*)

MARIE (*rising*)

Listen, daddy dear, and give me a serious answer —
which you never do when anybody speaks to you
about your health. How do you feel?

VIGNERON

Oh, not bad.

MARIE

But your face is red.

VIGNERON

Red! That 'll go away as soon as I get outdoors.

MARIE

If your dizziness comes back, we shall have to call
in a doctor.

VIGNERON

A doctor! Do you want me to die?

MARIE

You know that kind of joking hurts me. We won't
talk any more about it. (*She starts away, and he
catches her by the bottom of her gown and pulls her
down into his arms*)

VIGNERON

Does she love her old daddy?

MARIE

I love you so, so, so much . . . but you do.ı't do
a thing I want you to, or a thing you should do.
Why don't you work less, get some fun out of your
money, and look out for yourself when you are sick?

VIGNERON

But I am not sick, little girl. I know what 's the
matter with me. I 'm a bit tired, and there 's too
much blood in my head. It 's just the same every
year about this time, after I have finished taking

inventory.   The inventory of the house of Teissier,
Vigneron and Company! Do you know what Teissier
and I were offered for our factory, only a week
ago?   Six hundred thousand francs!

MARIE

Well, sell it.

VIGNERON

Ten years from now, I am going to sell for a million.
And in the meantime it will bring us in that much.

MARIE

How old will you be then?

VIGNERON

How old?   Ten years from now?   I shall be just
the age of my grandchildren; and we shall have fine
times together.   (*Auguste enters*)   What is it,
Auguste?

AUGUSTE

Your architect, sir.   He wants only a word with you.

VIGNERON

Tell Mr. Lefort if he wants to speak to me he should
see me at the factory.

AUGUSTE

He has just come from there, sir.

VIGNERON

Let him go back there.   I am at home here, with my
wife and children, and I shan't be bothered by my
contractors.   (*Auguste goes out*)   Let me get up.
(*Marie steps aside; Vigneron rises with an effort;
then he is seized with dizziness and walks a few steps
unsteadily*)

MARIE (*returning to him*)

Why won't you see a doctor?

VIGNERON

Isn't that question settled?

MARIE

No; it is not settled. There's no use talking — you are not well, and it makes me uneasy. Take care of yourself; do something; perhaps a little dieting for seven or eight days would make you all right again.

VIGNERON

Sly puss! I see through you and your little dieting. I eat too much, eh? Come, speak right out; I don't mind. I eat too much. Well, little girl, what do you expect? I haven't always had a table full of good things. Ask your mother; she will tell you that when we began keeping house I went to bed many a time without my supper. Now I'm making up for it. It's stupid, beastly, it hurts me, but I can't resist the temptation. (*Leaving Marie*) And then, I suppose I shouldn't read the newspaper after luncheon; it hurts my digestion. (*He crumples up the newspaper and going back to the couch throws himself upon it; then his glance falls upon Judith, who, seated at the piano, her back turned to her father, is in a brown study; he tiptoes over to her and shouts in her ear*) Judith!

JUDITH

Oh, father, you know I don't like such jokes!

VIGNERON

Don't be angry, missy, I won't do it again. Judith, tell me something about what's going on — in the moon.

JUDITH

Now make fun of me.

VIGNERON

How do you make that out? I have a daughter named Judith. Is she here? Is she somewhere else? How can I know? We never hear from her.

JUDITH

I haven't anything to say.

VIGNERON

That doesn't bother most people.

JUDITH

What fun is there in teasing me all the time about it? I see you, hear you, love you, and I am happy.

VIGNERON

Are you happy?

JUDITH

Quite.

VIGNERON

Well, then, little girl, you're right and I'm wrong. Have you got a kiss for me?

JUDITH (*rising*)

Have I? A hundred of them, daddy. (*They embrace; Auguste enters*)

VIGNERON

Now what is it? I don't seem to be able to kiss my children in peace, nowadays.

AUGUSTE

Mr. Dupuis, sir.

VIGNERON

Dupuis? Dupuis, the house furnisher? What does he want? I settled his bill long ago.

AUGUSTE

Mr. Dupuis stopped in to see if you wished anything, sir.

VIGNERON

Tell Mr. Dupuis for me that I don't buy twice of a swindler like him. Go ahead. (*Auguste goes out; Vigneron walks over to the table*) Well, what have you got your heads together about?

MRS. VIGNERON

Let us alone, that's a dear. We're busy with this evening's dinner.

VIGNERON

Oh! — Come and let me whisper just a few words in your ear. (*Mrs. Vigneron rises and joins her husband at the front of the stage*) So it's all settled that we are going to marry our daughter to that popinjay?

MRS. VIGNERON

Did you interrupt me just to say that?

VIGNERON

Now listen: I haven't any prejudice against this marriage. Mrs. de Saint-Genis impresses me as a first-rate woman. It isn't her fault if she hasn't a cent. Her son is a lovely little boy, very pleasant and polite, and he certainly does curl his hair nicely. For a long while, now, I've hardly been able to keep from telling him that he uses too much hair-oil. His government job carries a good salary with it, for a chap of his age. But at the last moment, I can't help wondering whether this marriage is well-advised, and whether Blanche will be really happy with that young fellow, even if he does belong to one of the oldest families.

MRS. VIGNERON

But Blanche is crazy about him.

VIGNERON

Blanche is only a child. It's easy to see that the first young fellow she met turned her head.

MRS. VIGNERON

What have you got up your sleeve? What's the use of talking that way about a marriage which is done and over with, one might say? You are n't reproaching me, are you, with Mrs. de Saint-Genis' financial position? Ours was n't always what it is now. Then what are you complaining of? Because George is a good-looking young fellow, well brought up, and of a good family? If he comes from one of the best families, so much the better for him.

VIGNERON

It flatters you to have a son-in-law from one of the oldest families.

MRS. VIGNERON

Yes, I admit it does flatter me; but I would n't sacrifice one of my girls to mere vanity. (*Coming nearer and speaking in a lower tone*) Do you want me to tell you the whole truth? It is true that Blanche is a child, as modest and innocent — the dear little girl — as can be; but her feelings are unusually powerful for a girl of her age, and we shan't regret having her married early. And then, our friend, Father Mouton, who has known us twenty years, would n't interest himself in the marriage if it were not for the best all around.

VIGNERON

Who said he would? But no matter, we are going ahead too fast. In the first place, it is n't a priest's business to make matches. And then, I'd like to have you tell me how it is that Mrs. de Saint-Genis

— who has n't a cent, I repeat — has such good connections. I thought that her son's witnesses would be commonplace people; gracious, she's found some smarter than our own! A high government official and a general! The government official I can account for — George works in his office — but the general!

MRS. VIGNERON

What's that? Oh, the general? Surely, you know that Mr. de Saint-Genis was a captain in the army. Run along to your work, dear. (*She turns away from him*) Blanche, give your father his coat. (*She goes out at the right, leaving the door open behind her*)

VIGNERON (*taking off his dressing-gown and putting on the coat brought by Blanche*) So here you are, you ingrate!

BLANCHE

Ingrate! Why do you call me that?

VIGNERON

Why? Now that we are rich, and are going to let you be married, and give you a dowry, why should n't we marry you to Mr. Teissier?

BLANCHE

No, papa.

VIGNERON

" No, papa." Why not? I reckon it's Teissier and his factory that have made me what I am.

BLANCHE

You mean that you have made Mr. Teissier's factory what it is. Without you, it would have cost him money enough; with you, heaven only knows how much money it has brought him in. Now see here, papa, if Mr. Teissier were anybody else — if he were a fair man — here is what he would say, after all the work you have done and the pains you have taken: This factory first belonged to me; then it belonged to both of us; now it belongs to you.

VIGNERON

Her kind little heart puts sentiment into everything. It's a good thing to have sentiment, but not to count too much on other people's having it. (*He kisses her*)

MRS. VIGNERON (*entering*)

What, are you still here?

VIGNERON

Answer this question: Am I under obligations to Teissier, or is Teissier under obligations to me?

MRS. VIGNERON

Neither.

VIGNERON

How is that?

MRS. VIGNERON

Do you really want me to go all over that story again?

VIGNERON

Yes.

MRS. VIGNERON

Well, children, Mr. Teissier was a banker in a small way, on the street where we used to live. We knew him, and yet we did n't. We had been under obligations to him at certain times when we were in need, and he had taken our note without much hesitation, because our reputation was good. Later on, in the course of his business, he found that he had a factory on his hands. He remembered your father and offered him the management, but with a salary. At that time we were getting along pretty well; your father had a good position with a good business house, and the wisest thing to do was to keep it. Fifteen months passed. We had thought nothing more of it for a long time, when one evening at exactly half-past nine — I remember the hour — when your father and I were looking through the door that led into your room, and watching you as you lay asleep, somebody rang. It was Mr. Teissier, and it was the first time he had ever climbed the five flights to our floor. He had made up his mind at last. The truth was, his works were not working, and he came to ask your father to come to his assistance by joining forces with him. Your father thanked him politely and asked him to wait till the following day for an answer. As soon as Mr. Teissier had gone, your father said to me — now listen to this — your father said to me: " Here is an opportunity, my dear. It comes rather late, and just when we are beginning to take things easy. It 's going to be a lot of work for me, and you will always be in a state of terror until I make a go of it — if I do make a go of it! But we have four children, and perhaps this is their chance." (*She weeps and clutches her husband's hand; the children gather around them, amid general emotion*) To come back to the question you asked, it seems to me easily answered. Mr. Teissier and Mr. Vigneron went into business together. It was a good thing for both of them, and they are quits.

VIGNERON

There, children! Does n't your mother tell it well?
Pattern after this woman, measure up to her stand-
ard, and nothing more can be expected of you. (*He
kisses his wife*)

MRS. VIGNERON

You do it beautifully, but it is n't natural to you,
my dear. Do you feel ill?

VIGNERON

No, sweetheart; on the contrary, I feel better. I
believe I have wholly recovered. Now I am going to
ask Miss Judith, the grrreat musician of the family,
to play me something, and then I 'll relieve you of
my company.

JUDITH

What do you want me to play? *Il Trovatore?*

VIGNERON

Find *Il Trovatore*. (*To Blanche*) That 's fine, that
Trovatore piece. Is it by Rossini?

BLANCHE

No; Verdi.

VIGNERON

Oh, Verdi, the author of the *Huguenots*.

BLANCHE

No; the *Huguenots* was written by Meyerbeer.

VIGNERON

That 's so. The great Meyerbeer. How old is
Meyerbeer, now?

BLANCHE

He 's dead.

VIGNERON

What? My goodness, did he die without my knowing
it? (*To Judith*) Can't you find *Il Trovatore?*

Never mind, don't take the trouble to look for it. Listen: play me — just play me — *La Dame Blanche*.

JUDITH

I don't know it.

VIGNERON

You don't know *La Dame Blanche?* Say that again. You don't know — ? What 's the good, then, of the lessons I 'm having you take at ten francs an hour? What *does* your music-teacher teach you? Tell me, now, what *does* he teach you?

JUDITH

He teaches me music.

VIGNERON

Well? Is n't *La Dame Blanche* music?

MARIE (*leading Judith to the piano*) Come, big sister, play daddy what he wants to hear. (*Judith seats herself at the piano and begins the famous selection*)

"From here behold that fair domain
Whose lofty turrets touch the sky;
A strange and spectral chatelaine
Guards that old castle ceaselessly.
Perfidious and faithless knight
Weaving your plots of shame and spite,
      Take care!
La Dame Blanche sees you there,
She hears — the woman in white!" [1]

---

[1] Translated by Allan Updegraff. The original is as follows:

> D'ici voyez ce beau domaine
> Dont les créneaux touchant le ciel;
> Une invisible châtelaine
> Veille en tout temps sur ce castel.

[*Vigneron begins to sing, then his wife joins him, then his daughters follow suit; half-way through the verse Gaston enters, having first stuck his head in at one of the rear doors. Then Gaston goes to the fire-place, takes the shovel and tongs, and contributes to the hubbub.*

VIGNERON (*going toward his son, when the verse is sung*) Where did you come from, you young rascal? Why were n't you at luncheon with us?

GASTON

I lunched with one of my friends.

VIGNERON

What 's that friend's name?

GASTON

You don't know him.

VIGNERON

I know well enough that I don't know him. Stand there while I have a look at you. (*He draws off a few steps, the better to survey his son. Gaston still has the shovel and tongs in his hands. Vigneron takes them away and puts them back in their place; then he goes back toward his son and regards him tenderly*) Stand up straight! (*He goes over to him and strokes his hair*) Show me your tongue! Good! Put it out a little farther. Farther than that. That 's all right. (*In a low tone*) I hope you 're not tiring yourself out too much.

> Chevalier félon et méchant
> Qui tramez complot malfaisant,
>   Prenez garde!
> La dame blanche vous regarde,
> La dame blanche vous entend!

GASTON

Doing what, dad? I have n't been doing anything.

VIGNERON

Now you 're talking nonsense. When I said " You 're
not tiring yourself out too much," I knew what I
meant, and so did you, you scamp. Do you need any
money?

GASTON

No.

VIGNERON

Open your hand.

GASTON

What 's the use?

VIGNERON (*speaking louder*)

Open your hand.

GASTON

I don't want to.

VIGNERON

Papa Vigneron brought this boy up, so he did!
Here, put this money in your pocket, and be quick
about it! Have a good time, kid — I want you to
have the best kind of a time. Cut loose and raise the
dickens. But remember — away from here you are
your own boss — but here, among your sisters, mind
how you act! Be careful what you say; and above
all, no mushy letters! If you want to confide in anybody, I 'm the one.

JUDITH

We 're waiting for you to join in the second verse,
dad.

VIGNERON (*looking at his watch*)

You 'll have to sing the second verse without me.
(*He takes his hat and goes toward the door. Then,*

*pausing and looking around at his family, he comes
back like a man who is happy where he is, and does
not want to go away*) Come here a minute, old lady!
(*Mrs. Vigneron comes over to him, and he puts one
arm under hers*) Judith, get up! (*He does the
same to Judith*) Come here, you other girls! If I
had my own way, dearies, I'd get back into my
dressing-gown and stay here until dinner time. But
unfortunately my work won't do itself; and I have n't
money enough yet to live without working. Perhaps
I shall have some day, when I am the owner of the
factory. But I must wait for two things — till my
new buildings are finished, and until my children are
provided for. Who could have thought that this
little minx Blanche, the youngest of you, would be
the first to get married? Whose turn is it next?
Judith? Oh, Judith is a young lady hard to please.
Unless she meets a prince, she 'll die an old maid.
Well, then, let some prince come along, and I 'll buy
him for her. As for you, you young scamp, standing over there laughing while I am talking — you
can have your fling, but it won't be for long. Some
fine day I 'm going to take you to work with me, and
you are going to start in by sweeping the factory,
from top to bottom — until I make an errand boy
of you. After that we 'll see whether you are good
for anything. Of you all, I 'm the least worried
about Marie. She is n't a dreamer (*looking at
Judith*) like you; nor a sentimentalist (*looking at
Blanche*) like you. She 'll marry some good fellow,
some healthy chap, a hard worker and tough as a
knot, who will make you think of your father when
he 's not here any more. (*To his wife*) I have n't

mentioned you, sweetheart, because at our age, we don't have any great longings or needs. We 're happy if the kids are happy. I don't think these children of ours would have been any happier anywhere else. Well, and what next? Just let the old man put in a few more years to ensure the future of this little family, and then he 'll have earned the right to take a rest. Now, then, I 'm off!

THE CHILDREN

Good-bye, papa. Kiss me. Good-bye. (*Vigneron escapes from them and goes out quickly*)

MRS. VIGNERON

Now, girls, get yourselves ready. (*To Blanche*) I want you to wait a minute; I 've got something to say to you. (*To Marie*) Look in at the kitchen, dear, and tell Rosalie to be sure not to keep us waiting; hurry her up a little. Rosalie is very fond of us, but she 's always late with dinner. Gaston, let your sister go to her room — you can take your music lesson some other time. (*There is a hustle and bustle as all the children except Blanche go out*) Now pay attention, dearie; I have n't time to talk much. I want you to make use of what I 'm going to tell you; and don't interrupt me. I don't like the way you conduct yourself when your future husband is here. You look at him too much; when he gets up, you get up; you get into little corners to do your talking. I don't like those things; and to-day, when we have visitors, I should like it less than ever. If you admire George, and if you love each other, so much the better, since you are going to be married — but you are not married yet. Until you are, I want you to be more careful, and I want you

to keep your feelings to yourself, as a nice girl
should do. There's no sense in crying about it!
It's all said and done. Now dry your eyes, give
me a kiss, and go and get yourself ready. (*Blanche
leaves her mother and is going out at the door when
Auguste enters at the rear and announces Mrs. de
Saint-Genis; Blanche pauses*) Go and get ready!

MRS. DE SAINT-GENIS

How do you do, dear. Come, kiss me. It's not only
the style, it's a perfect mania now, for people to
kiss every five minutes. I'm here early, but don't
let me disturb you. If I bother you the least bit,
just say so. I'll stay or go, just as you please.

MRS. VIGNERON

Oh, stay, by all means.

MRS. DE SAINT-GENIS

Perhaps you have calls to make?

MRS. VIGNERON

Not one.

MRS. DE SAINT-GENIS

Then maybe you expect to receive some?

MRS. VIGNERON

No.

MRS. DE SAINT-GENIS

Shall I take off my hat?

MRS. VIGNERON

If you don't I'll put mine on.

MRS. DE SAINT-GENIS

It isn't often nowadays, Mrs. Vigneron, that one
finds a woman like you — a woman who can be seen
any time. I wouldn't want to risk such a thing with
some of my most intimate friends.

MRS. VIGNERON

Sit down and tell me how you feel.

MRS. DE SAINT-GENIS

I 'm well; quite well. I don't remember ever feeling
better. I was saying this morning, at my toilet,
that I had got back my color and figure.

MRS. VIGNERON

There is a question I 've been wanting to ask you,
ever so long. It should n't make any difference between us. How old are you?

MRS. DE SAINT-GENIS

Why, Mrs. Vigneron, I never try to hide my age.
Even if I wanted to, I could n't; on account of my
son. He will be twenty-three years old in a few
days; I was seventeen when he was born; you can
figure it out.

MRS. VIGNERON

Then you don't mind my curiosity?

MRS. DE SAINT-GENIS

It is quite natural, between two old women.

MRS. VIGNERON

You know we are two rash mothers — you, in letting
your son marry so young, at twenty-three, and I in
letting my daughter marry him!

MRS. DE SAINT-GENIS

Don't worry about that, my dear. George has
obeyed me so far, and I certainly count on keeping
him straight after he is married. I have brought
up my son very strictly, as I think I have already
told you, and there are few children like him. He
has never gone into debt; and what is just as un-
usual, he has never frittered away his time with

women. All the same, I know some women who
would n't have asked anything better. My son has
had a very thorough education; he speaks three
languages, he plays, he bears a good name, has good
manners and religious principles. So, with all that,
he won't go far wrong, unless the world changes a
good deal. (*Changing her tone*) Tell me, now that
we are talking about George, and since I am looking
out for his interest, does your husband know that I
asked my lawyer to rectify an omission in the marriage contract?

MRS. VIGNERON

I can't say as to that.

MRS. DE SAINT-GENIS

You remember that Mr. Vigneron, after having fixed
Blanche's marriage portion at two hundred thousand
francs, asked us to let him pay it in the form of an
annuity.

MRS. VIGNERON

That 's not so, Mrs. de Saint-Genis. From the very
first my husband said that he wanted time to settle
his daughter's dowry. It was then that you spoke
of some guarantee, a mortgage on the buildings under
construction; and he refused to do that. Finally,
the amount and the time of payment was fully agreed
upon.

MRS. DE SAINT-GENIS

Very well. It seemed to me only natural and fair
that until the young couple come into the whole sum,
it should pay them interest of five or six per cent —
say, six per cent. However, in making out the contract Mr. Vigneron showed such kind spirit toward

all my little whims, that there will be no trouble between us. Let us talk about something else. Your
dinner, for instance. Are you going to have many
here?

MRS. VIGNERON

There are your witnesses, and ours, and my eldest
daughter's music-teacher —

MRS. DE SAINT-GENIS

Oh, you have invited him —

MRS. VIGNERON

Yes; we invited the young fellow. He is a musician,
I know; but really we did n't want to make him feel
his position.

MRS. DE SAINT-GENIS

Well, Mrs. Vigneron, perhaps you will think I am
meddling with what does n't concern me, but if I
were in your place I 'd let him come this once, and
then see no more of him.

MRS. VIGNERON

Why, Mrs. de Saint-Genis? My daughter has never
had reason to complain either of him or his work.

MRS. DE SAINT-GENIS

Well, never mind. Who else is there?

MRS. VIGNERON

Mr. Teissier — that 's all.

MRS. DE SAINT-GENIS

So I am going to meet this Mr. Teissier, whom I
have heard so much of, but whom I have never yet
seen! (*She rises and goes over to Mrs. Vigneron,
taking her by the hand in a friendly way*) Why is
it, Mrs. Vigneron, we have never seen your husband's
partner?

MRS. VIGNERON

My daughters don't like him.

MRS. DE SAINT-GENIS

Surely your daughters do not lay down the law in your house? I should think Mr. Vigneron would have his partner come here regardless of childish whims.

MRS. VIGNERON

But the men see each other every day at the factory, and when they have talked over their business affairs, they have nothing more to say to each other.

MRS. DE SAINT-GENIS

Now see here, Mrs. Vigneron, I am not the kind of a woman to betray anybody's confidence; but if I guessed a secret, that would be different. Now own up — for some reason or other, it 's you who have kept Mr. Teissier from coming here.

MRS. VIGNERON

I? You are entirely wrong about that. In the first place I do whatever my family wishes; besides, if I don't exactly like Mr. Teissier, at least I don't absolutely dislike him.

MRS. DE SAINT-GENIS

You — just feel indifferent toward him?

MRS. VIGNERON

That 's exactly it — indifferent.

MRS. DE SAINT-GENIS

Then I must say that you are either very short-sighted, or altogether too unselfish. Is n't Mr. Teissier extremely wealthy?

MRS. VIGNERON

Yes.

MRS. DE SAINT-GENIS

And past sixty?

MRS. VIGNERON

Long past.

MRS. DE SAINT-GENIS

He has no wife or children.

MRS. VIGNERON

That's right.

MRS. DE SAINT-GENIS

It is n't known that he has a mistress?

MRS. VIGNERON

A mistress! Mr. Teissier! Good Lord, what would he be doing with a mistress?

MRS. DE SAINT-GENIS

Now listen; it's no laughing matter. Here you have, right in your grasp, a big unclaimed legacy which may come any day. It could fall to you without making talk and without underhanded means. Does n't such a legacy mean anything to you? Either you don't care for money, or you think that it would be buying it too dearly if you showed some semblance of affection for an old man.

MRS. VIGNERON

What you say is true enough, Mrs. de Saint-Genis, and you are not the first one who has said as much. I'll explain my position. If we should be indebted to a stranger, our home would n't be quite the same; my husband could n't hold up his head, and we should n't be as happy. But this reason does n't apply to you. There's nothing to keep you from trying your luck with Mr. Teissier, after the children are married. If he takes an interest in this marriage,

so much the better. I would be only too glad if
Blanche and her husband could benefit in that way.
Well, I'm drifting away from the point. If Mr.
Teissier, who must be tired of living alone at his
age, should succumb to your charms, I should be
quite pleased to see you married to him. Of course,
there would be certain disadvantages on your side,
but the compensations would be great.

MRS. DE SAINT-GENIS

You don't know men, Mrs. Vigneron, and you're
talking nonsense. In a pinch, Mr. Teissier would n't
be too old for me; the trouble is I'm not young
enough for him.

AUGUSTE (*entering*)

Mr. Merckens has just come, ma'am. Shall I show
him into the other parlor?

MRS. VIGNERON

Which would you rather do, Mrs. de Saint-Genis —
stay here and talk with Mr. Merckens or come and
help me dress?

MRS. DE SAINT-GENIS

Just as you please.

MRS. VIGNERON

Then come with me. I'll show you some things
I have bought, and you must tell me whether they
are the latest style.

MRS. DE SAINT-GENIS

With pleasure.

MRS. VIGNERON

Bring Mr. Merckens in and ask him to wait a few
moments. (*They go out at the left*)

AUGUSTE

Come in and have a chair, Mr. Merckens. I 'm the only one here just at the moment.

MERCKENS

All right; go ahead with your work, Auguste; don't let me disturb you. (*Going down the stage*) The servant is a good fellow, but this treatment is intolerable.

AUGUSTE (*coming back again*)

No lessons to-day, Mr. Merckens. You 're here to have a good time.

MERCKENS

Is Miss Judith dressing?

AUGUSTE

Probably. But you know, with her it 's one, two, three — done!

MERCKENS

Please tell Miss Judith that I 'm here and have brought the music she wanted.
[*At this moment Judith enters.*

AUGUSTE

Now what did I tell you! (*To Judith*) You were n't long dressing, miss, but you put in your time pretty well.

JUDITH

Thank you, Auguste.
[*Auguste takes up Vigneron's dressing-gown and goes out.*

MERCKENS

Your servant took that compliment out of my mouth; now I don't know what to say.

JUDITH

Well, it is n't worth while bothering about.

MERCKENS (*unrolling some sheets of music*)
Here is your composition, Miss Judith.

JUDITH
Let me have it.

MERCKENS
The name of the composer is n't on it, but I can have it put on.

JUDITH
You must keep it to yourself.

MERCKENS
Are you satisfied?

JUDITH
I don't know what to do. I know so well that the family, and particularly mama, would n't like our little conspiracy.

MERCKENS
I repeat what I told you about this little piece. It is distinctive and interesting. It 's a little bit melancholy; perhaps you had a cold in the head that day. We had it printed because it was worth it; that 's all there is to it.

JUDITH
Now understand, Mr. Merckens, I reserve the right to show my composition or to say nothing about it, just as I please.

MERCKENS
Why?

JUDITH
Because a girl of my age must live very quietly, without letting herself indulge in unbecoming fancies.

MERCKENS
The young ladies I know are not so particular.

JUDITH

All the more reason. (*She opens the music and reads the title tenderly*) " Farewell to the Bride and Groom." I 'm not surprised that this piece is sad. I felt deeply while I was writing it. I was thinking of my little sister whom we all love so much and who is so soon to leave us. Who knows what she is giving up, and what fate awaits her!

MERCKENS

To tell the truth, was n't there something under-handed about this marriage?

JUDITH

No. Why do you ask?

MERCKENS

Mrs. de Saint-Genis had her pick. She could have asked for the oldest rather than the youngest.

JUDITH

That would have been too bad. He and my sister make a fine couple, and that would n't have been the case — otherwise.

MERCKENS

Don't be impatient; your turn will come.

JUDITH

I don't let that worry me.

MERCKENS

Yet you do wish a little that you were married?

JUDITH

As late as possible. I 'm getting along first-rate, and I don't care to make any change.

MERCKENS

Composing satisfies you?

JUDITH

You are right, it does.

MERCKENS

It seems too bad that such a delightful young woman, so gifted, should lack just a little something which would make her work worth while.

JUDITH

What is that something?

MERCKENS (*in a low tone*)

A little of the devil.

JUDITH

Mama would n't be pleased if she heard you say that; she 'd think I was already running wild.

MERCKENS

Does your mother scold you sometimes?

JUDITH

Yes, sometimes. But worse than that, when she is angry she locks up my piano; and she has told father not to take us to the Opera.

MERCKENS

Where do you go, then?

JUDITH

To the Circus. I don't blame mama, though. She thinks the Opera is bad for me; and perhaps she is right. It 's true; the wonders of the scenery, the allurement of the acting, and the splendid singing — why, it 's a week before I am myself again.

MERCKENS

These great singers get high prices, you know.

JUDITH

They are all great to me.

MERCKENS

Perhaps you envy them?

JUDITH

I 'm wild about them.

MERCKENS

Why don't you be one?

JUDITH

What! I go on the stage?

MERCKENS

Why not? You have a good contralto voice, and there are very few contraltos. You have the presence, and vivacity, and, above all, you have feeling — a great deal of it. The world will never miss one housekeeper, and it will rejoice in one more artist.

JUDITH

Hush! don't say any more about it. I am going to stick to your lessons. They seem to me better than your advice. Have you an engagement for this evening? Will you stay a little while after dinner?

MERCKENS

A little while. I still count on hearing your composition.

JUDITH

And you will play something for us, too?

MERCKENS

Don't ask that. I don't stand on ceremony with you; you and I speak right out. When I am talking I can be witty and amusing; but my music does n't resemble my conversation the least bit.

JUDITH

We 're going to dance.

MERCKENS

Nonsense!

JUDITH

Yes, we are. Blanche wanted to. The least she can do is to dance once or twice with her future husband before she is married. And then Gaston has a sur-

prise for us. He insists he is going to dance a
quadrille with his father, and that we won't be able
to tell them apart.

MERCKENS

How so?

JUDITH

You 'll see. You don't know how my brother can
imitate papa to the very life. It 's wonderful how
much like him he seems at those times — his voice,
his gestures, his way of joking.

MERCKENS

I can see you are going to have a good time. Thank
you for asking me to be here.

JUDITH

Now you 're making fun of me, Mr. Artist. I don't
want to be too severe, but I fancy that many of your
parties are n't worth all the fuss you make about
them. Our folks would consider them ridiculous, too,
to say the least. There 's one thing we can say, anyway; here you will be among respectable people.
(*Mrs. Vigneron and Mrs. de Saint-Genis reënter*)

MRS. DE SAINT-GENIS (*aside*)

I knew we 'd find them together. (*Judith goes over
to her and they greet each other affectionately*)

MRS. VIGNERON (*dressed loudly and covered with jewelry*) Pardon me, Mr. Merckens, for making you
wait. Women never do get dressed. Do you think
I look well?

MERCKENS

Dazzling!

MRS. VIGNERON

Perhaps I have too much jewelry on. Mrs. de
Saint-Genis advised me to take off some of it.

MERCKENS

Why, Mrs. Vigneron? Princess Limperani wore
three hundred thousand francs' worth at the dinner
she gave yesterday.

MRS. VIGNERON

Three hundred thousand francs! Then I can keep
on what I have.

[*Marie and Blanche enter.*

MRS. VIGNERON (*going to Judith*)

Your father is late. He won't be here to receive his
guests.

BLANCHE (*to Mrs. de Saint-Genis*)

Why did n't your son come with you?

MRS. DE SAINT-GENIS

George is working, dear. You must n't expect me to
keep him from his duties.

BLANCHE

He has more than one kind of duty now. He must
love me as much as I love him.

MRS. DE SAINT-GENIS

That 's easy. He won't have to forget his other
duties to do that. I warn you we are going to pull
hair if you begin to spoil my boy.

MRS. VIGNERON (*to Mrs. de Saint-Genis*)

I suppose George's witnesses will arrive together.

MRS. DE SAINT-GENIS

No. Mr. Lenormand and my son will leave the office
and come here together; the general will come alone.
The general and Mr. Lenormand know each other,
because they have met at our house, but I have never
tried to bring about any closer relationship between
them.

AUGUSTE (*announcing*)

Mr. Teissier!

TEISSIER (*entering*)

How do you do, Mrs. Vigneron.

MRS. VIGNERON

Let me take your hat, Mr. Teissier.

TEISSIER

Never mind. I 'll put it somewhere myself, so as to be sure of finding it again.

MRS. VIGNERON

Just as you like. Won't you sit here, in this armchair?

TEISSIER

I will in a few minutes. It 's so cold outdoors and so warm in here that I 'm going to stay on my feet until I get used to the temperature of the room.

MRS. VIGNERON

I hope you are not ill?

TEISSIER

I try to keep from being ill.

MRS. VIGNERON

How do you think my husband has been lately?

TEISSIER

Very well. Vigneron takes better care of himself, now that he 's got some money ahead. He 's right, too. A man's life is worth more when he 's got something laid by. You can attend to your guests, Mrs. Vigneron; I 'll sit in the corner until dinner time. (*He leaves her*)

MRS. VIGNERON (*going over to Mrs. de Saint-Genis*)

Well, that 's Mr. Teissier! What do you think of him?

MRS. DE SAINT-GENIS

He has the eyes of a fox and the face of a monkey.

AUGUSTE (*announcing*)

Mr. Bourdon!

MRS. VIGNERON

I forgot to tell you that our lawyer will dine with us.

BOURDON

How do you do, ladies — young people — (*Greetings*)

MRS. VIGNERON (*presenting Bourdon*)

Mrs. de Saint-Genis; Mr. Merckens, my eldest daughter's music-teacher. You are one of the first to come, Mr. Bourdon; that's very nice of you. (*Bourdon bows*)

MRS. DE SAINT-GENIS

Mr. Bourdon is setting a good example for his brother lawyers. They don't usually pride themselves on their punctuality.

BOURDON

Yes, we do sometimes keep people waiting — but never at dinner. (*Going over to Mrs. de Saint-Genis*) I have been asked to congratulate you, Mrs. de Saint-Genis.

MRS. DE SAINT-GENIS

Mr. Testelin?

BOURDON

Yes. We were talking about your son's marriage to Miss Vigneron, and I happened to say that I was going to have dinner with you. "There will be a delightful woman there," he said. "Give her my best regards."

MRS. DE SAINT-GENIS

Mr. Testelin has been my lawyer for twenty years.

BOURDON

So he said. (*In a lower tone, coming nearer to her*)
Testelin is a courteous fellow, with considerable weakness for pretty women.

MRS. DE SAINT-GENIS (*dryly*)

It 's the first time I ever heard that. (*She leaves him,
smiling*)

BOURDON (*to Mrs. Vigneron*)

Is Teissier dining here?

MRS. VIGNERON (*pointing out Teissier to him*)

There he is, if you want to talk to him.

BOURDON

How are you, Teissier?

TEISSIER

Oh, it 's you, Bourdon! Come here a minute; I
want to tell you something. (*In a low tone*) I was
at the Lawyer's Club to-day on business. I was
speaking to the President about my long acquaintance with you, and he got rather confidential about
you. "I know Bourdon," he said. "He 's got
brains enough; he 's as shrewd as they make them;
but sometimes he overplays his hand. We 've got to
squelch him."

BOURDON

What do I care for the Lawyer's Club? They 're a
crowd of stiff-necks who want to give the Club a
goody-goody tone. The Club is meant to be a pro-
tection for us — not for the public.

TEISSIER

Now listen, Bourdon; I have n't repeated this conversation to keep you from doing business. I just
thought I would be doing you a favor by letting you
know.

BOURDON

So I take it, friend Teissier. I 'm much obliged.

AUGUSTE (*announcing*)

Mr. Lenormand and Mr. George de Saint-Genis!

MRS. DE SAINT-GENIS (*to Mrs. Vigneron*)

I want you to meet Mr. Lenormand. (*This presentation and those following take place at the rear.
George alone goes to the front of the stage*)

BLANCHE (*speaking in a low tone to George*)

Don't say anything to me, and don't come too near
me. Mama has given me a dressing down. I was
terribly afraid; I did n't know just what she was
going to say.

AUGUSTE (*announcing*)

General Fromentin!

BOURDON (*to Merckens*)

You are a pianist?

MERCKENS

A composer.

BOURDON

A musician — that 's what I should have said. Do
you like to go into society?

MERCKENS

I can't help myself; I 'm dragged into it.

BOURDON

You might remember my name and address, " Mr.
Bourdon, lawyer, 22 St. Anne street." We have a
few friends with us every Sunday evening. I ought
to warn you there 's nothing fancy about it. The
people come at nine o'clock, we have a little music,
sing a few songs, have a cup of tea, and by midnight everybody is in bed.

MERCKENS

I could n't promise to come every Sunday.

BOURDON

Come when you can; we 'll be glad to see you any
time.

AUGUSTE (*announcing*)

Mr. Vigneron!

MRS. DE SAINT-GENIS (*to Mrs. Vigneron*)

What! Is your husband in the habit of announcing
his arrival?

MRS. VIGNERON

The servant has made a mistake, of course.
[*Gaston enters, with his father's dressing-gown on.
He imitates his father's voice and walk.*

GASTON (*approaching Mrs. de Saint-Genis*)

How is the lovely Mrs. de Saint-Genis?

MRS. DE SAINT-GENIS (*taking the joke in good part*)

I 'm very well, thank you, Mr. Vigneron.

GASTON

Mr. Bourdon, I am your humble servant. (*To
Merckens*) How do you do, young man. (*To
Lenormand and the General*) Delighted to meet you,
gentlemen.

MRS. VIGNERON

That 's what we get for spoiling children! This
young rascal is caricaturing his father.

GASTON (*to Mrs. Vigneron*)

Well, old lady, is dinner ready? By heavens, we
have n't spared any expense to give you a good time;
we don't have a marriage in the family every day.
(*To his sisters*) Which one of you is it? I don't
remember. It strikes me that while we are waiting

for dinner Miss Judith ought to play us something
— *La Dame Blanche*, for instance.

MRS. VIGNERON

Come, Gaston, that 's enough. Take off that dressing-gown and act properly.

GASTON

Yes, old lady. (*The sisters help him off with the
gown, amid general laughter*)

AUGUSTE (*approaching Mrs. Vigneron*)

There 's a gentleman here who was n't invited to dinner and wants to speak with you.

MRS. VIGNERON

What gentleman, Auguste? Is this some new joke
of my son's?

AUGUSTE

If you order me to admit him you will see whether
it is or not.

MRS. VIGNERON

Don't admit anyone. Tell the gentleman I can't see
him.

AUGUSTE

If he insists, ma'am?

MRS. VIGNERON

Then send him about his business.

AUGUSTE (*returning*)

Here he is, ma'am.

THE DOCTOR (*coming forward*)

Mrs. Vigneron?

MRS. VIGNERON

Yes, sir.

THE DOCTOR (*coming close to her and speaking in a
very low voice*) Have you children here, Mrs.
Vigneron?

MRS. VIGNERON
Yes, sir.

THE DOCTOR
Send them out of the room. Please do it at once.

MRS. VIGNERON (*disturbed, and speaking quickly*)
Go into the other parlor, girls. Run along, now; do as I tell you; go into the other parlor. Gaston, you go along with your sisters. Mrs. de Saint-Genis, will you please take the girls in? (*She opens the door at the right, and the children pass out*)

THE DOCTOR (*speaking to the men, who have risen*)
You can stay, gentlemen. Are you relatives of Mr. Vigneron?

BOURDON
No, just his friends.

THE DOCTOR
Well, gentlemen, your friend has just had a stroke of apoplexy.
[*Vigneron is brought in at the rear. Mrs. Vigneron cries out and throws herself upon her husband's body.*

CURTAIN

THE SECOND ACT

The scene is the same as in the preceding act.

MRS. VIGNERON (*weeping, with handkerchief in hand*)
Do forgive me, Mrs. de Saint-Genis; I'm ashamed to weep like this before you, but I can't help it. To think that only one month ago he was sitting there right where you are now, and that I shall never see him again! You knew him; he was so good, so happy; he was too happy, and so were we all; it could n't last. Do talk to me; it will give me a chance to control myself. I know I ought to make the best of it. He had to die sometime. But many a time I used to ask God to let me be the first to go. Don't you think men as good as my husband go to heaven?

MRS. DE SAINT-GENIS
There 's no doubt about it, Mrs. Vigneron.

MRS. VIGNERON
Tell me about your son. I have scarcely laid eyes on him since our misfortune. He 's good, too; Blanche told me he wept.

MRS. DE SAINT-GENIS
George is well, thank you.

MRS. VIGNERON
What a setback it is for the poor dears! And they love each other so much!

MRS. DE SAINT-GENIS

This marriage is exactly what I should have talked of if I had found you composed. You are not sensible or courageous, my dear. I know what it is to lose a husband. I 've been all through it. Only I had more reason to complain than you. When Mr. de Saint-Genis died he left me nothing but debts and a four-year-old child on my hands. Your daughters are old enough to be a consolation to you; they are grown up; and you don't have to worry about their future or your own. (*Changing her tone*) I suppose now, in the condition you are in, you have n't given thought to your business affairs?

MRS. VIGNERON

What business affairs?

MRS. DE SAINT-GENIS

You ought to know that Mr. Vigneron's estate won't settle itself. You will have to have the apportionment settled, and perhaps there will be some difficulties to meet.

MRS. VIGNERON

Oh, no, Mrs. de Saint-Genis, no difficulties. My husband was too honest a man ever to have business difficulties.

MRS. DE SAINT-GENIS

They could arise after his death. Now listen to me. It is n't Mr. Vigneron's uprightness I 'm questioning; it 's that of the other people. Have you seen Mr. Teissier yet?

MRS. VIGNERON

Mr. Teissier has stayed at home as usual. I needed money, and he sent it to me after a little urging; that is the extent of our dealings.

MRS. DE SAINT-GENIS

Now listen to what I tell you, Mrs. Vigneron. Even if my advice should be wrong in this case, adopt it as a general rule: Keep an eye on Mr. Teissier.

MRS. VIGNERON

All right, I will keep an eye on him. But just suppose he should have bad intentions: it's my lawyer, not I, who should bring him to terms.

MRS. DE SAINT-GENIS

Keep an eye on your lawyer.

MRS. VIGNERON

Oh, Mrs. de Saint-Genis!

MRS. DE SAINT-GENIS

There's no use saying "Oh!" I know these lawyers, Mrs. Vigneron. You never know whether they are going to save you or be the undoing of you; and according to their ideas you are always in the wrong.

MRS. VIGNERON

What would you say if I should tell you that my lawyer, Mr. Bourdon, is also Mr. Teissier's lawyer?

MRS. DE SAINT-GENIS

I would advise you to get another.

MRS. VIGNERON

No; I have a blind confidence in Mr. Bourdon, and I shan't get rid of him till I lose it.

MRS. DE SAINT-GENIS

It will be too late then.

AUGUSTE (*entering and speaking to Mrs. Vigneron*)

Mr. Lefort sends his regards and wants to know if you have looked over his memorandum.

MRS. VIGNERON

His memorandum! Did he give me one?

AUGUSTE

Yes, ma'am.

MRS. VIGNERON

Where did I put it?   I don't know anything about it.

AUGUSTE

Mr. Lefort will call sometime during the day.

MRS. VIGNERON

Very well, tell him I will see him.   (*Auguste goes out*)   Mr. Lefort is our architect.

MRS. DE SAINT-GENIS

Keep an eye on your architect!

MRS. VIGNERON

I don't know where you got such a bad opinion of other people, Mrs. de Saint-Genis; but if I were you, I should n't display it.

MRS. DE SAINT-GENIS

It's the least I can do to put you on your guard. Everybody looks honest to you.

MRS. VIGNERON

And nobody looks honest to you.

MRS. DE SAINT-GENIS (*rising*)

I don't wish you any harm, Mrs. Vigneron, and I hope with all my heart, for your sake and the sake of your daughters, who are really delightful girls, that everything goes smoothly in settling Mr. Vigneron's estate.   But in business nothing goes smoothly.   What seems simple is complicated, and what seems complicated is beyond understanding. Take my word for it, you will be wise to stop thinking a little while of him who is gone, in order to think of yourself and your children instead.   Unfortunately I don't know whether Mr. Vigneron left you an annuity or government bonds.   He did n't, did he?

I dare say his fortune was in that factory, owned by
him and Mr. Teissier together? He had land, true
enough; but he had bought most of it with borrowed
money and on mortgage. I tell you all this with the
best of feeling. Women ought to warn and help each
other. As for self-interest, it looks as though I no
longer had any. We had a very nice plan, to marry
our children. I must say it is not merely postponed,
but really in danger. It does n't seem possible for
you to fulfil the financial obligations you undertook,
and I would n't let my son make a poor marriage for
anything — and have him blame me for it afterwards.

MRS. VIGNERON

Just as you please, Mrs. de Saint-Genis. (*A pause
and embarrassed silence*)

MRS. DE SAINT-GENIS (*speaking quickly*)

Good-bye, Mrs. Vigneron. Do as I tell you; look
out for your interests, and we can talk about our
children some other time. But for heaven's sake,
Mrs. Vigneron, get this into your head — it is the
most useful and the friendliest advice I can give you:
Keep an eye on everybody — *everybody!* (*She goes
toward the door at the rear, Mrs. Vigneron coldly
escorting her. The door opens and Teissier enters*)
Stay here; you need n't go to the door with me.
(*She goes out*)

MRS. VIGNERON (*weeping, handkerchief in hand*)

What a terrible thing this is, Mr. Teissier! My
poor husband! It was work that killed him! Why
did he work so hard? He did n't care for money;
he spent nothing on himself. Oh, he wanted to see
his children happy while he was living, and to leave
them rich! (*A silence*)

TEISSIER

Mrs. Vigneron, did you authorize Mrs. de Saint-Genis to come to my house to find out how things stand in regard to your husband's estate?

MRS. VIGNERON

I know nothing about it, and I should not have sanctioned it.

TEISSIER

I did my duty on the double-quick. I took the lady by the arm and showed her the door.

MRS. VIGNERON

That's all she deserved. Mrs. de Saint-Genis was here when you came, Mr. Teissier, and was talking about my husband's affairs. You know all about them and understand them better than anybody else. Won't you enlighten me?

TEISSIER

When I have a few minutes of leisure, I'll take pleasure in drawing up a statement of your husband's estate. What do you want most to know? Whether it will be settled at a loss or profit? (*Mrs. Vigneron waves her hand deprecatingly*) From off-hand calculations I have made, the situation in general looks something like this — now pay attention: when the factory is sold —

MRS. VIGNERON

Why sell it?

TEISSIER

We shall have to. When your real estate and the unfinished buildings also, are sold —

MRS. VIGNERON

I'm going to keep my real estate.

TEISSIER

You can't. When your current debts are liqui-
dated —

MRS. VIGNERON

But I have no debts.

TEISSIER

I figure them at about forty thousand francs. In
that sum I have n't included your architect, who will
have to be paid after your real estate is sold. Let
me go on. After the registry tax is paid —

MRS. VIGNERON

What! Does a person have to pay for inheriting
money?

TEISSIER

Certainly you have to pay, Mrs. Vigneron. Now,
when the usual expenses have been met — I include
under the head of "usual expenses" such things as
the lawyer's fees, and those of his associates, unfore-
seen bills, carriage hire, postage, etc. In a word,
when you have closed the account which you must
open under the head of "Settlement of the estate of
the late Mr. Vigneron, my husband" there will be
left about fifty thousand francs.

MRS. VIGNERON

Fifty thousand francs a year income.

TEISSIER

What, income? Don't you hear what I 'm telling
you? How do you see in what Vigneron left the
capital necessary to provide an income of fifty thousand francs?

MRS. VIGNERON (*leaves him abruptly, and, having rung,
opens the writing-desk in a hurry and writes*) "My
dear Mr. Bourdon. Please come and see me as soon

as you can. I shall not rest easy till I have seen
you. Mrs. Vigneron." Fifty thousand francs! (*To
Auguste, who has just come in*) Deliver this letter
at once.

TEISSIER (*having taken out a pocketbook cram full of
papers*) Now if you will pay better attention while
I am reading —

MRS. VIGNERON

Fifty thousand francs! (*Turning to Teissier and
making him stuff the papers back into his pocketbook*) Keep your papers, Mr. Teissier; I want nothing more to do with you. (*She goes out at the left
hurriedly*)

TEISSIER (*stuffing the papers back*)

Ignorance, incompetence, impulsiveness — that's a
woman, all over. What's she thinking of, I'd like
to know? She wants to keep her lands. Well, she
can't. Bourdon will have to make her understand
that. If Bourdon can handle this case as he promised
me he could — quickly and quietly — I can get my
hands on real estate worth twice what it will cost
me. But we can't lose a minute's time. Delay will
bring around a crowd of prospective buyers, and that
puts prices up. When Bourdon finds out that I
have struck the first blow, he'll do the rest in a hurry.
(*He is going out when Marie enters at the left*)

MARIE

Don't go away, Mr. Teissier, before making up with
my mother. She has cried so much, poor thing, that
she does n't know which end her head is on.

TEISSIER (*coming back*)

You stopped me just in time, young woman. I was
going to have your mother summoned into court, in

order to recover the money I have advanced to her.
For my part, I'd rather not leave your mother in
this mess. (*He takes out his pocketbook again and
selects a different paper from it*) Please give your
mother this little bill. She can verify it easily
enough: " On the seventh of January, advanced to
Mrs. Vigneron 4000 francs to pay the expenses of
your father's funeral; on the fifteenth of January,
advanced to Mrs. Vigneron 5000 francs for household expenses "; (at least, that's what she said it
was for); " on the same day " — the fifteenth, understand? — " paid out, in taking up a bill of exchange signed by your brother and drawn to the
order of a money-lender named Lefébure, 10,000
francs." Your brother being under age, his signature was worthless. But your mother, knowing that
your brother deceived the man about his age and personal resources, did n't want the money-lender to be
cheated. (*He folds up the paper and puts it back in
the pocketbook*) Now, what can I do for you?

MARIE

Please stay awhile, Mr. Teissier. It was n't this bill
that upset my mother and made her lose her temper
with you. On the contrary, she would have thanked
you for honoring my brother's signature. She put
the blame on him, where it belongs.

TEISSIER (*surprised, and smiling*)

Then you know what a signature is?

MARIE

My father told me.

TEISSIER

He would have done better by telling your brother.

MARIE

Sit down, Mr. Teissier. Perhaps I am rather young to talk business with you.

TEISSIER (*remaining standing, smiling all the while*)

Go ahead, talk; I'm listening.

MARIE

Speaking for myself, I am looking for a great change in our social condition, but I don't think that we shall lose everything. In any case, Mr. Teissier, you would not advise us to be either too yielding or too rash, would you? Then what are we to do? Why, we must find out just where we stand, ask for advice, and not take a single step without knowing the why and wherefore of our condition.

TEISSIER

Ah! — Leaving aside the real estate, which does n't concern me, what would you do with the factory, while you are waiting?

MARIE

What will happen, Mr. Teissier, if we want to keep it, and you want to sell it?

TEISSIER

It will be sold. The law provides for such a case.

MARIE

There is a law about it?

TEISSIER (*smiling all the while*)

Yes, miss, there is a law on the subject. Article 815 of the Statutes authorizes either one of two partners to dissolve a partnership that has been broken by the death of one of them. I can prove it to you on the spot. (*Taking a book from his pocket*) You see the title of this book: " Collected

Laws and Regulations in Force throughout French
Territory." I always carry a copy with me. I
advise you to do the same. (*He passes her the book
with a certain page indicated. While she is reading
he watches her with a look in which are mingled interest, pleasure and mockery*) Do you understand
it?

MARIE

Perfectly. (*A pause*)

TEISSIER

Your name is Marie, and you are the second
daughter?

MARIE

Yes, Mr. Teissier. Why?

TEISSIER

Your father had a marked preference for you.

MARIE

My father loved all his children alike.

TEISSIER

Nevertheless he considered you cleverer than your
sisters.

MARIE

He used to say so sometimes, to console me for not
being as good-looking as they are.

TEISSIER

What's the matter with you? You have pretty eyes,
rosy cheeks, a well-rounded figure, everything that
goes to indicate a healthy woman.

MARIE

I am not worried about my appearance. All I ask
is not to be noticed.

TEISSIER

Of course, you are the one that helps your mother run the house. In a pinch you would make a good private secretary.

MARIE

There has never been any necessity for it so far.

TEISSIER

Now is the time. I don't believe your mother is capable of disentangling herself alone. You will be a great help to her. Have you any taste for business?

MARIE

I understand as much of it as I have to.

TEISSIER

You 're not afraid to take care of correspondence?

MARIE

No; I know what has to be said.

TEISSIER

Are you good at figures? Come, yes or no? You don't want to tell? (*Leaving her*) She ought to be a wonder at figures.

MARIE

Mr. Teissier, what do you think our real estate is worth?

TEISSIER

Your lawyer can tell you that better than I can. (*Going back toward her, after taking up his hat*) I must get back to business now, miss. I know what you are thinking of; that the factory is a fine property, and you can keep a hold on it. Who is going to assure me that it won't fall down some night? Who is going to convince me that you yourselves, by

some slick trick, might not sell it so that you could
buy it up at half price?

MARIE

Why should you anticipate that, Mr. Teissier?

TEISSIER

I anticipate only what I would do myself, if I were
forty years old instead of sixty odd. To sum up,
your need of money on the one hand, and on the
other hand my knowledge of where my best interests
lie, are going to end in the sale of the factory. Its
condition is very prosperous. The death of its man-
ager is a good excuse, and one that does n't often
happen along, to sell out at a profit. Have you got
anything else to say to me?

MARIE

Don't go away, Mr. Teissier, without seeing my
mother again. She is calmer now, and will listen
to you very willingly.

TEISSIER

It 's no use. I told your mother what I had to say.
You are intelligent enough to explain the rest to her.

MARIE (*having rung*)

Do what I ask, Mr. Teissier. My mother could not
help losing her temper; by going in to see her, you
will give her a chance to apologize.

TEISSIER

Well, just as you say. So you want us to be on
good terms? I 'll tell you right now, you can't gain
anything by it. How old are you, Miss Marie?
Scarcely turned twenty! And already a modest,
sensible little woman, who is able to express herself

very clearly. (*Leaving her*) And what her father did not tell me, a very tempting creature. (*Auguste enters*)

MARIE

Go with Auguste, please; he will take you in to my mother.

TEISSIER

My best wishes for you, miss. (*He goes out at the left, at a signal from Auguste to follow him*)

MARIE (*bursting into tears*)

Oh, father, father!

BLANCHE (*entering and going slowly over to her sister*)

What's the matter, dear?

MARIE

Mr. Teissier.

BLANCHE

Is it that scoundrel you've been with such a long while?

MARIE

Hush, dear, hush. We must be careful now and not talk indiscreetly.

BLANCHE

Why?

MARIE

Why? I don't want to tell you; but whether you know to-day or to-morrow, it will be just as hard for you.

BLANCHE

What do you mean by that?

MARIE

We may be ruined.

BLANCHE

Ruined!

[*Marie lowers her head. Blanche burst into tears,
and the two girls put their arms around each other.
Then they separate, but Blanche continues to weep,
and is greatly affected.*

MARIE

I should n't have told you about a misfortune that
may not happen. Here is the whole truth: I don't
yet see very clearly into our situation, but it does n't
look promising. Nevertheless, it may all come out
right, on one condition: that we are reasonable, prudent, careful in our dealings with everybody, and
make up our minds from this moment to overlook
many distasteful things.

BLANCHE

You can do as you please, mama, Judith and you;
but I shall have nothing to do with it. I should like
to sleep until after I am married.

MARIE

Until after your marriage, dear!

BLANCHE

Now what have you on your mind?

MARIE

I 'm sorry to think that this marriage, which means
so much to you, may not take place, after all.

BLANCHE

You are wrong, if you think Mr. de Saint-Genis
thinks more about a dowry than he does about a
loving heart.

MARIE

Men want both when they marry. But even if Mr.
de Saint-Genis were the most disinterested man in the

world, he has a mother who will do the calculating
for him.

BLANCHE

His mother is his mother. If she has faults, I don't
want to see them. But she has been married, and she
would not want her son to be disloyal to another
woman.

MARIE

Let's not be unreasonable and unjust in our misfortune, dear. Both families have promised certain
things; if we cannot keep ours, Mr. de Saint-Genis
will be released from his.

BLANCHE

You are wrong, you are wrong, I am sure of it. If
I should say the word to-morrow, or a year from now,
or ten years from now, George would marry me, just
as he ought to do, if I wished it. You see, dear, my
marriage is not like so many others, which can take
place or not, without doing harm. You don't know
how you are hurting me by having the least doubt
about its taking place. (*Pause*) Tell me something
about how we are ruined.

MARIE

Later on; I don't know myself, yet.

BLANCHE

Who told you about it?

MARIE

Mr. Teissier. I must tell you again to be careful.
Mr. Teissier is in the other room with mama. I
have just made it up between them.

BLANCHE

Were they angry with each other?

MARIE

Yes, they were. Mama lost her temper and told him to get out.

BLANCHE

She did right.

MARIE

She did wrong; and she knew it right away. Our situation is bad enough without making it worse by hasty and thoughtless actions. Bear in mind, Blanche, the very existence of all of us, you as well as the rest of us, is at stake. No matter how sure you may feel of Mr. de Saint-Genis, a man looks twice before marrying a woman who has n't a cent. You are the sweetest little woman in the world; you are all heart and feelings; for you money does n't exist; but you will find it exists for other people. You will find that out wherever you go. In business, for instance; and we are engaged in business with Mr. Teissier. In marriages, too, as perhaps you are going to learn to your cost. Money certainly has its price. Otherwise there would not be so many misfortunes coming from the lack of it, or so many vile deeds committed because of it.

BLANCHE (*aside*)

Is it possible that a young man like him, loving and beloved as he is, would stoop to such a base act rather than sacrifice his money interests?

MARIE

You know what I would like, don't you, dear? You know I want this marriage to take place, because you see happiness in it. But if I were in your place, I should be prepared for anything. I should be in

raptures if it took place; and if it did n't I should
be resigned.

BLANCHE

Resigned! If I thought that Mr. de Saint-Genis
had sought me out for my money, I should n't be
able to hold up my head again. And if he refused to
marry me because I had lost my money, I should
either go crazy or I should die.

MARIE

Then you do love him a great deal?

BLANCHE

Yes, I do. If you want to know, I worship him!
He is kind and loving, and childlike, just as I am.
I am positive he has a big heart and could n't bring
himself to do a wrong thing. You can see, can't
you, how much I want to marry him? But even if
I should be deceived in him; if I should find out that
he was not worthy of either love or respect; if he
should prove to be the vilest creature in the world,
I should still have to marry him —

MARIE (*aside*)

The poor girl is suffering so much she does n't know
what she is saying.

BLANCHE (*aside*)

Oh, what have we done that is wrong? — You know
me, sister dear. We have lived together for twenty
years without any secrets from each other. Have n't
I been a good girl? I have been very affectionate, I
know; but have n't I been good, too? I have never
had a single thought that I could n't tell. If I had
met Mr. de Saint-Genis in the street, I should n't
have even looked at him. But he came here arm in
arm with my father. We liked each other immedi-

ately, and so we were engaged. Mama told me to keep an eye on the future, but I could n't see any great harm or wrong in trusting him.

MARIE

Come, don't go on that way; you are exaggerating, as you always do. You told Mr. de Saint-Genis that you loved him, I suppose? Well, you are going to marry him, so that 's excusable. You held hands sometimes? Perhaps you let him kiss you? You should n't have done that; but it does n't call for all the reproaches you are heaping on yourself.

BLANCHE (*after a little hesitation*)

I am his wife, do you hear? I am his wife!

MARIE (*very innocently*)

I don't see what you mean.

BLANCHE (*at first overcome with amazement*)

Oh, forgive me, dearie. You are as pure as an angel. I should n't have spoken to you that way. Forget what I have just said; don't try to understand it; and please don't say anything about it to mama or Judith.

MARIE

Either you are slightly out of your head or I am rather stupid.

BLANCHE

Yes, that 's it; I am out of my head. And you are the dearest and sweetest sister anyone ever had. (*She kisses her passionately*)

BOURDON (*entering*)

How do you do! Your mother is in, is n't she? Will you please tell her that I am here?

MARIE

You go, dear. (*Blanche goes out at the left*)

BOURDON

Your mother just wrote me that she was very eager
to see me; and I can readily believe it. I have been
at my office every day, waiting for her to call me.

MARIE

My mother has been so afflicted, Mr. Bourdon, and
has suffered so much —

BOURDON

I understand perfectly, my dear young lady, that a
woman who has had such a blow as your mother
can't enjoy paying visits or going shopping. But
it is no more than proper to see your lawyer, or at
least to ask him to drop in. Fortunately, your
father's estate does not offer very great difficulties.
Nevertheless, your father left considerable real estate
which ought to be inspected at once and turned into
cash as soon as possible. Understand me, as soon as
possible.

MARIE

Here 's mother.

MRS. VIGNERON (*weeping, handkerchief in hand*)

What a terrible blow, Mr. Bourdon! What a dreadful thing! My poor husband! I don't seem to be
able to weep enough. I just know I shall never live
through it. (*A silence*)

BOURDON

Tell me, Mrs. Vigneron, while I happen to think of
it: did you give Mrs. de Saint-Genis permission to
call on me to learn how things stand in regard to
your husband's estate?

MRS. VIGNERON

She had no permission from me. And so Mrs. de
Saint-Genis paid you a visit, too —!

BOURDON

Don't worry about that. The way I treated her she won't want to come again. You wanted to see me, Mrs. Vigneron. Please speak quickly and clearly, and make it brief.

MRS. VIGNERON

I won't detain you long, Mr. Bourdon. I have only one question to ask you. Is it true — is it possible that my husband left all told only fifty thousand francs?

BOURDON

Who told you that?

MRS. VIGNERON

Mr. Teissier.

BOURDON

Fifty thousand francs! Teissier was too quick about it. You know him; he is n't a bad man, but he is brutal when it comes to a matter of money. I hope you will get more than that out of it, Mrs. Vigneron, and I will do all I can, you may be sure. (*Mrs. Vigneron bursts into tears and sinks upon the couch; Bourdon goes over to her*) So, you were hoping that Mr. Vigneron's estate would amount to a great deal? What was your estimate?

MRS. VIGNERON

I don't know, Mr. Bourdon.

BOURDON

But you should have figured up what your husband left. When a woman loses her husband, that 's the first thing she should think of. (*He walks away*) However, it was none the less wrong on Teissier's part — and I 'll tell him so, too — to name an

amount at random.   Business is n't conducted that
way.   In a settlement, the way to begin is at the
beginning, taking up the most urgent matters; then
advancing step by step until the end is reached —
and then you have what you have.   (*Returning to
Mrs. Vigneron*)   Have you made any decision, Mrs.
Vigneron, about your real estate?   There your necessity is manifest; it must be sold.

MARIE

How much do you think it would bring us?

BOURDON (*going over to Marie*)

How much?   Nothing.   You can't count on anything.

MRS. VIGNERON (*rising*)

Then what is the advantage in getting rid of it?

BOURDON (*returning to Mrs. Vigneron*)

What advantage, Mrs. Vigneron?   By doing so you
remove the shackles from your feet.   Believe me, I
am not usually so downright in my advice as I am
at this moment.   Each day's delay is filled with
grave consequences for you.   While you are deliber-
ating, Catiline is at the gates of Rome; Catiline being, in this case, the mortgages that are eating you
up, your architect with his bill, and the civil authorities, with their taxes and fees.

[*Teissier reënters at the left; Blanche comes in behind him.*

TEISSIER

How are you, Bourdon?

BOURDON

How do you do, Teissier.   I was just explaining to
Mrs. Vigneron and her daughter the impossibility of
their holding on to their real estate.

TEISSIER

I have nothing to say as to that. The ladies could n't
find a better adviser than you. They are in good
hands.

BOURDON

Mrs. Vigneron, please look at the thing from my
point of view, so that we won't misunderstand each
other. I don't want to be reproached later on for
what was n't my fault. I restrict myself to this
principle: the *statu quo* being deadly against you,
you must get rid of the *statu quo*. I can't say that
your real estate is well situated, or that this is the
best time to put it up at auction. Far from it.
But, by having the sale at the most favorable time
— and I'll look out for that — and getting rid of
certain obstacles, together with some smooth work
and clever advertising, we may get something good
out of it.

TEISSIER (*aside*)

What's that? What's that? (*In a low tone to
Bourdon*) Then we're not working together in this?

BOURDON (*in a low tone to Teissier*)

Let me go ahead. (*Going over to Mrs. Vigneron*)
Now, then, Mrs. Vigneron, think it over; but think
it over quickly, I urge you. When you have made
up your mind, please let me know. (*He makes a
move as if to go*)

TEISSIER

Don't go, Bourdon, without saying something about
the factory.

BOURDON

The factory can wait, friend Teissier. I want to
help Mrs. Vigneron get rid of her real estate before

we do anything else. We see here a widow and four
children who are growing poorer every day. That's
a mighty important state of things; we must n't forget that.

[*Teissier smiles.*

AUGUSTE (*entering, and in a low voice to Mrs. Vigneron*) Mr. Lefort is here, ma'am.

MRS. VIGNERON

Please wait a minute, Mr. Bourdon. After hearing
what our architect has to say you may change your
mind.

BOURDON

Just as you say, madam.

MRS. VIGNERON (*to Auguste*)

Bring Mr. Lefort in, and ask Judith to come here.

[*Lefort enters.*

MRS. VIGNERON (*weeping, her handkerchief in her hand*)
What a terrible blow, Mr. Lefort! What a dreadful
thing! My poor husband! I shall never get over
his loss.

LEFORT (*he has vulgar manners and a powerful voice*)
Come, madam, don't cry like that. With a little
nerve and perseverance you can fill your husband's
boots. (*He goes up stage*)

TEISSIER

Hello, Lefort!

LEFORT

Glad to see you, Teissier.

[*Judith enters.*

MARIE (*to Lefort*)

Were you very much interested, Mr. Lefort, in the
buildings entrusted to you?

LEFORT

Yes, miss. Vigneron was more like a brother than a client.

MARIE

We are on the eve of making an important decision —

LEFORT

Ask me anything you want to. My time is yours, my money is at your service. Vigneron's children are my children.

MARIE

If you had some explanations, or even some project, to let us hear, please tell us in the presence of these gentlemen.

LEFORT

I am ready, miss. These gentlemen don't scare me. It's a way of mine to stand right up to everybody.

MRS. VIGNERON

Sit there, Mr. Lefort.

LEFORT (*seated*)

Have you looked at my memorandum, madam? No? That's bad. It contained a little account of Mr. Vigneron's real estate, showing the whole business from A to Z. If I had that account right here before me, I could be briefer and make you understand better.

MARIE

I can give it to you, Mr. Lefort. I put it away myself.

LEFORT

If you please.

[*Marie goes to the writing-desk, passing in front of her mother and Teissier, who are seated side by side.*

TEISSIER (*to Mrs. Vigneron*)

Is your daughter methodical?

MRS. VIGNERON

Very.

TEISSIER

She's likely to grow up to be a clever woman, is n't she?

MRS. VIGNERON

Yes, I think so.

TEISSIER

Is she good at figures? (*No reply*)

BOURDON (*having taken the memorandum from Marie, he detaches part of it and hands it to Lefort*) That's what you want, undoubtedly. If you don't mind, I'll run over your memorandum while I am listening to you. (*The two men exchange hostile glances*)

LEFORT (*stressing each phrase*)

In the first place, Mr. Vigneron's real estate, situated on the outskirts of Paris near a railway station, and on that account under a thousand disadvantages, was, at the price he paid for it, a sorry bargain. To speak plainly, he was a sucker.

BOURDON

Stop! Nobody had any reason to deceive Mr. Vigneron. He bought this land hoping it would be taken by eminent domain.

LEFORT

By whom?

BOURDON

By the railroad.

LEFORT

Great joke, that is! It was the railroad that sold it to him.

BOURDON

Are you sure of that?

LEFORT

Absolutely sure.

BOURDON

Well, even so. Then he must have supposed that the city, which had undertaken some big work in the neighborhood, would need that land. I remember, now; he expected to do business with the city.

LEFORT

Huh! With the city or with the Turks! You can't tell me anything about real estate. I know the lay of Paris land from A to Z. Well, I'll go on. Mr. Vigneron having been caught for a sucker — I say it again — very quickly realized his foolishness and wanted to dodge the consequences. How could he do it? By building on the land. Then he sent for me. He knew of old that I was square and straight-forward, and before I left him he had given me the work of making plans. Unfortunately I had scarcely begun the work, and the foundations had hardly been laid (*he accompanies his words with a comical panto-mime*) when Vigneron moved on to the next world.

BOURDON

We know all these details, my dear fellow. You are wasting our time in telling them over again.

LEFORT

The heirs are in a bad fix; but they can get out of it and make something, too. They can command the services of a man who is faithful, intelligent and highly esteemed throughout the building profession in Paris. That man is the architect who served the deceased. He is now their architect. Will they listen to him? If they ignore his advice and management (*another comical pantomime*) their goose is cooked.

BOURDON

Now, sir, cutting out phraseology, what's your plan?

LEFORT

Let's reason it out from the least favorable hypothesis. Leave Lefort out of it. He put in an honest bill, without quibbling over each item. He asked for nothing more for himself. Now what's going to become of the real estate? I repeat that it is situated far from the centre of the city, and I add that it suffers from numerous other defects. It is encumbered with mortgages. These are just so many points which some unknown purchaser could turn against the owners. (*Volubly*) It would be like this: somebody would depreciate the property, precipitate a public sale, get rid of any honest prospective buyers, fool the courts into granting a judgment at some miserably small sum, pack the auction (*more pantomime*) and there you have a property reduced to nothing.

BOURDON

I demand, sir, that you be more precise. You say somebody would do this, that and the other. Who would do it, pray? Do you know that only one person could do it, and that you are slandering the lawyer who has charge of the settlement of the estate?

LEFORT

That's you, ain't it?

BOURDON

I am not speaking for myself, sir, but for all my
brother lawyers, whom you are libelling. You are
attacking, offhand, the most respectable body of men
I know of. You are bringing under suspicion the
Law itself, in the persons of the officers sworn to
execute it. Sir, you are doing worse, if it be possible. You are disturbing the security of families.
Really, now, it 's rather stiff to make an accusation
like this, and then bring in a bill of thirty-seven
thousand francs!

LEFORT

I should like to be present when you present *your*
bill.

BOURDON

Enough, sir! Now, briefly, what do you propose?

LEFORT

I 'm coming to my proposal. I propose that the
Vigneron heirs carry out the building —

BOURDON

Well, now, that 's what I thought you were getting
at. You are the architect, and you propose to continue the building operations.

LEFORT

Let me go on, sir.

BOURDON

It is n't worth while. If Mrs. Vigneron wants to
listen to you, she may; but I can't bear such ram-
bling talk any longer. How much money can you
sink in it? Mrs. Vigneron has no money; of that I
warn you. Where is yours? In three months we
should be back at the same point, with this difference

— that your bill, now thirty-seven thousand francs,
would be doubled, at the rate you are going. Don't
force me to say any more. I take your offers in
the spirit they are made. I don't want to witness
any such shady transaction, which would hand the
ownership over to you for a song.

LEFORT

Do you know what you are saying, sir? Look me in
the eye. Do I look like a man who would indulge
in shady transactions? Upon my soul, I never saw
such a clown as you in my life.

BOURDON (*restraining himself, and speaking just above
a whisper*) What did you call me, you humbug!
(*Mrs. Vigneron rises to intervene*)

TEISSIER

Let 'em go on, madam; don't say anything. Never
interrupt a business conversation.

LEFORT (*to Mrs. Vigneron*)

I give in, madam. If you want to know my plan and
the resources at my disposal, you can call me again.
In the other event, you will please settle my bill as
soon as possible. I have to advance money to my
clients; while lawyers juggle with their clients'
money. (*He goes out*)

TEISSIER

Wait for me, Lefort. We'll go up street together.
(*To Mrs. Vigneron*) I leave you in Bourdon's
hands, Mrs. Vigneron. Profit by his advice.

LEFORT (*returning*)

I forgot to say, madam — was it with your permission that Mrs. de Saint-Genis came to my
place — ?

MRS. VIGNERON

She has been everywhere! I gave nobody permission to go to see you, Mr. Lefort; nobody. And if she comes again —

LEFORT

She won't. She went down the stairs quicker than she came up.

TEISSIER (*to Marie*)

Good-bye, Miss Marie, and good health to you. (*He leaves her, and then comes back*) Stay as you are. You won't lack lovers. If I were not so old, I'd get in line. (*He and Lefort go out together*)

BOURDON

Well, madam?

MRS. VIGNERON

What have I done, Mr. Bourdon, to have such a scene?

BOURDON

I shall not regret that discussion, madam, if it shows you where your interests lie.

MRS. VIGNERON

Putting aside what has just passed, let's look at things as they are. I agree that Mr. Lefort is a man who lacks good breeding, but he has a good deal of common sense and a knack of getting things done. After all, what he proposes is nothing more than what my husband would have done, if he had lived.

BOURDON

Are you serious, madam, in what you are saying? Haven't you learned to appraise that architect's offers at their real value?

MRS. VIGNERON

By taking somebody else we could —

BOURDON

You are not satisfied yet? (*A pause*) Come here,
young ladies; you are not in the way. Your mother
is wandering in cloudland; help me get her back on
earth. Mrs. Vigneron, I am going to present the
matter in its best light. Admitting, for the sake
of argument, that the real estate belongs to you —
forgetting the creditors and mortgagees who have
claims on it — do you know what it would cost to
finish those buildings of yours, of which the foundations have hardly been put in? Four to five hundred
thousand francs! You know well that Mr. Lefort
has n't that amount. You cannot count on me to
get it for you. And then, even if you could get it
through me or anyone else, would it look well for a
woman, I ask, to place herself at the head of a large
establishment and throw herself into an enterprise
that nobody could see the end of? This question
that I am asking you is so serious that if it were
brought up before the civil authorities, whose duty
it is to help you bring up your minor children, it
could be opposed on the ground that the childrens'
inheritances — what little they have — were being
risked in mere speculation. (*Speaking solemnly*)
As a member of that civil board, pledged to look out
for the best interest of minor children — the greatest
duty in existence — I should oppose it myself.
(*Silence*) Take heed, madam. I will not overstep
the bounds of my duty by saying anything more.
You know where my office is; I will await further
orders there. (*He goes out*)

MRS. VIGNERON

Let's talk awhile, children.   Don't all speak at once, and try to listen.   Mr. Lefort —

JUDITH (*interrupting*)

Oh, Mr. Lefort!

MRS. VIGNERON

You don't know yet what I was going to say.   Perhaps Mr. Lefort did express himself very clumsily, but I believe he has a good and loyal heart.

JUDITH

I don't believe so.

MRS. VIGNERON

Why?

JUDITH

I think he has the manner of a swindler.

MRS. VIGNERON

Oh!   And you, Blanche; do you think Mr. Lefort has a swindler's manner?

BLANCHE

Yes, somewhat.   I agree with Judith.

MRS. VIGNERON

So!   Anyhow, his advice seems better to me than Mr. Bourdon's.   All Mr. Bourdon's amounts to is that we shall sell our property.   What do you think, Marie?

MARIE

I have n't anything to say just yet.

MRS. VIGNERON

We're making splendid headway, are we not? — Well, then, what do you think about Mr. Teissier?

MARIE

It seems to me that if we don't offend him, but show him a little regard, we may get help from Mr. Teissier.

BLANCHE

What's that, Marie?   Mr. Teissier is the most treacherous and dangerous man in the world.

MRS. VIGNERON

Judith?

JUDITH

I don't know who is right, Marie or Blanche; but the way I look at it, we can't count on getting help from anyone but Mr. Bourdon.

MRS. VIGNERON

I don't agree with you, dear.   Mr. Bourdon!   Mr. Bourdon!   There is one question that Mr. Bourdon should have asked me right off, and he never seemed once to think of it.   Then I noticed something obscure about his words.   What did he mean by saying: "Catiline is at the gates of Rome"?   (*To Marie*)   Did you understand that?

MARIE

Yes, I understood it.

MRS. VIGNERON

You did?   Is that so?   We won't talk about it any more; you are wiser than I am.   But Mr. Bourdon could have spoken to me about Catiline some other time.   Why did n't he ask if we needed money?   Now listen, children.   If we must sell the real estate, we must.   What we shall lose, we shall lose.   But remember what your mother says; once and forever, as long as I live: they shall *not* touch the factory.

MARIE

You are wrong there, mama.

MRS. VIGNERON

As long as I live they shan't touch the factory!

MARIE

Mr. Teissier could sell it to-day. He has a legal right to do it.

MRS. VIGNERON

As long as I live —

MARIE

There is a law —

BLANCHE AND JUDITH

If there is a law!

MRS. VIGNERON

Come, don't bother me about your law. If I should go through many days like this, I could n't stand it; you would soon be without either father or mother. (*She falls upon the couch, weeping*)

AUGUSTE (*entering*)

Here are some letters for you, ma'am.

MRS. VIGNERON (*to Marie*)

Take these and read them, dear.

MARIE

This one is a letter from your dressmaker: "Dear Madam. We take the liberty of sending you your bill, and beg to remind you that it has passed the ordinary credit limit. Our cashier will call upon you to-day. Believe us, madam, yours very truly. P. S. May we call your attention to a brand new dress goods called 'short-term mourning,' which looks well on young women, and can be worn by misses with equally good effect." (*She opens and reads another letter*) "Dear Madam. Mr. Dubois hereby gives you permission to sub-let your apartment, which will not be difficult, provided you make a small sacrifice. Mr. Dubois would like to do more,

but he cannot. If he should permit you to break
a lease on account of the death of the lessee, he
would be establishing a precedent which would cause
him much trouble." (*Third letter*) "Dear Madam.
I sent to your house last week concerning my bill
against you, and my young lady representative was
rudely treated by your servants, and could not make
collection. Not being able to reach you, I do not
know how to understand a delay which must not be
further prolonged. I do not run after business, and
as you know, madam, I do not advertise in the papers;
I leave that to the big Parisian houses that charge
you more on that account. If I am able to make hats
at a surprisingly low price, at the same time showing originality and superior workmanship, it is
merely because of my large business and regular col-
lections."

[*Marie prepares to read a fourth letter. Mrs. Vigneron stops her and begins to weep. The young
girls look on without a word, with bowed heads,
saddened and frightened.*

CURTAIN

THE THIRD ACT

The scene is the same as in the first and second acts.

ROSALIE

Sit down, ma'am.

MRS. DE SAINT-GENIS (*hesitating and annoyed*)

I don't know.

ROSALIE

Do as I tell you, ma'am. Sit down there and be comfortable, with your pretty little feet on this hassock.

MRS. DE SAINT-GENIS

Don't urge me, Rosalie. I am wondering whether it would be wiser to wait or to come again.

ROSALIE

Do as I say, ma'am. Wait. You'll get me in trouble with Blanchy if I let you go away without seeing her.

MRS. DE SAINT-GENIS

Blanche will see me a little later. She is just the one I came to see, and I want to talk to her about a very serious matter. I did n't think Mrs. Vigneron would have company at luncheon.

ROSALIE

Not company; no, there 's no company.

MRS. DE SAINT-GENIS

The ladies of the house are at luncheon; is that what you mean?

ROSALIE

Yes.

MRS. DE SAINT-GENIS

They are not alone, are they?

ROSALIE

No.

MRS. DE SAINT-GENIS

Then there is somebody with them?

ROSALIE

Yes. (*In a low tone*)   Mr. Teissier.

MRS. DE SAINT-GENIS

Oh, Mr. Teissier!   (*Coming close to Rosalie*)   He comes here now, does he?

ROSALIE

Oftener than folks like to have him.

MRS. DE SAINT-GENIS

But they give him a welcome?

ROSALIE

They have to.   The young ladies are right in not liking him, but the need of being on good terms with him overcomes that feeling.

MRS. DE SAINT-GENIS

On good terms with him?   What for?

ROSALIE

For the sake of their fortune.

MRS. DE SAINT-GENIS

Yes, Rosalie, for the sake of their fortune (*moving away*) or for his.

ROSALIE

You 're going to stay, are n't you, ma'am?

MRS. DE SAINT-GENIS

No, I 'm going.   I 've made up my mind.   Mr. Teissier is here, and the ladies have business with

him. What business? I don't want to embarrass
anybody, or pry into any secrets. (*She goes toward
the door*)

ROSALIE

Will you call again, ma'am?

MRS. DE SAINT-GENIS

I 'll call again.

ROSALIE

Surely?

MRS. DE SAINT-GENIS

Surely. Listen, Rosalie. If Mrs. Vigneron and her
daughters — except Blanche, you understand — wish
to go out, let them go; don't let them put themselves
out for me. Blanche is the only one who need wait
in for me. I want to speak with her once and for all.
You are her old nurse; so you tell her to keep calm
— to think it all over — to make up her mind to the
inevitable — that it is n't my fault that her father is
dead — that she must take into account her financial
condition — and my son can't be responsible — that
he can't — not by any means — Now, Rosalie, do
you understand what I 'm asking you to say?

ROSALIE

Certainly I understand, ma'am. But you must n't
expect me to say anything that would distress my
little Blanchy.

MRS. DE SAINT-GENIS

There, that 's your bell. See what 's wanted, and
I 'll find my own way out. (*She leaves*)

ROSALIE

She gives me the creeps, that woman does. I cross
myself every time she comes in and goes out.

[*The third door at the rear opens. Teissier comes in with Marie on his arm, and Mrs. Vigneron behind them. Then comes Judith, and finally Blanche. Rosalie steps aside to let them pass; she stops Blanche, arranges her dress and embraces her, then goes out through the open door, closing it behind her.*

TEISSIER

Do you mind if I lean on you a little? I 'm not used to eating so much at luncheon, and with such nice people. (*Stopping*) What did I say at the table?

MARIE

Different things.

TEISSIER

What about?

MARIE

About life in general.

TEISSIER

Did we say anything about your affairs?

MARIE

The subject did n't come up. (*They proceed, going toward the right; then Marie disengages herself and walks away*)

TEISSIER (*following her*)

Your sisters are nice; the oldest one especially is well built. Yet I prefer you. I have n't always been old. I can still tell a blonde from a brunette. I 'm very much pleased with you, understand?

MARIE

Pay a little attention to my mother.

TEISSIER

Why is it, Mrs. Vigneron, that Gaston, the boy that writes such fine I O U's, did n't have luncheon with us?

MRS. VIGNERON (*with some emotion*)

My son is engaged.

TEISSIER

He's gone soldiering. That's the best thing he could do. A soldier is lodged, fed and warmed at the expense of the government. What risk does he take? None but being killed. And then he does n't need anything.

MRS. VIGNERON

My son did what he wished; but he will be sorry for it later. I wanted to arrange with you, Mr. Teissier, to put him in the factory; and if the factory, as I believe, does n't go out of your hands or ours, Gaston would take his father's place in a few years. (*Silence*)

TEISSIER

Have you seen Bourdon?

MRS. VIGNERON

No. Should we see him?

TEISSIER (*embarrassed and making no reply, but turning to Marie*) Your sisters are nice; but they are city women. You can see that at a glance. No color. Looking at you, nobody would ever say that you had been brought up with them. In the summer I have roses in my garden, but they have n't the bloom your cheeks have. You and your mother and sisters must come and visit my country house. You are no longer children, so you won't hurt anything. You can have luncheon at home before you start, and be back in time for dinner. You have n't many diversions; that will be one for you.

MARIE

You must n't expect us to come to see you, Mr. Teissier, before our position is easier. You know we have n't progressed a bit, just got more tangled up, that 's all. We are being tormented now by our old tradesmen. They have become very impatient creditors.

TEISSIER (*embarrassed, and making no reply, but turning to Mrs. Vigneron*) If you want to go on with your work, madam, don't bother about me. Your girls will keep me company until I go.

MRS. VIGNERON

Stay as long as you please; we shan't send you away. (*Going over to Marie*) Have you spoken to Mr. Teissier?

MARIE

No, not yet.

MRS. VIGNERON

Are you ashamed to?

MARIE

Yes, I am ashamed to. Twelve thousand francs is a big sum to ask for.

MRS. VIGNERON

Let 's not ask for it.

MARIE

And where shall we be to-morrow if that dressmaker puts her bill in the hands of a sheriff? She will do just as she said.

MRS. VIGNERON

Do you want me to take Mr. Teissier aside and save you from doing it?

MARIE

No. This is the time to show courage, and I am going to show it.

TEISSIER (*seated on the couch beside Judith*)

Do you get along well with your sisters?

JUDITH

Very well.

TEISSIER

Who is the cleverest of you three?

JUDITH

Marie.

TEISSIER

Miss Marie. (*He looks at her*) Does she think very much about getting married?

JUDITH

She never says anything about it.

TEISSIER

Yet people think she is pretty.

JUDITH

She is more than pretty; she is charming.

TEISSIER

Exactly. (*He looks again at Marie*) She is n't a living skeleton, like so many of the young girls, and she is n't a heavyweight, either. Has she a firm character?

JUDITH

Very.

TEISSIER

Simple tastes?

JUDITH

Very simple.

TEISSIER

Is she the kind of a woman who would stay at home and like to take care of an old person?

JUDITH

Maybe.

TEISSIER

Could a person give her the keys of a house, without being uneasy about it? (*Judith looks at him in astonishment*) Then what's she thinking of? Why does n't she have a talk with me? (*Rising and speaking to Judith*) I don't want to keep you, miss. Go over there (*pointing at Blanche*) where your sister is sitting, looking as though she were doing penance. (*Marie approaches him. He joins her and they come out to the front of the stage*) What do you call that little thing you have there?

MARIE

Just a purse.

TEISSIER

What for?

MARIE

A charity bazaar.

TEISSIER

For the poor? I see. You 're working for them while they are loafing.

MARIE

Mr. Teissier, my mother wants me to ask something of you that she herself does n't dare to ask.

TEISSIER

What is it?

MARIE

As I was telling you just now, it seems that our tradesmen have got their heads together. Where we once could n't get them to send in their bills, now it is a question of which can get his money first.

TEISSIER

These people are within their rights in claiming their due.

MARIE

Unfortunately we have n't the amount necessary to
settle with them. A pretty round sum. Twelve
thousand francs. Mr. Teissier, please lend us this
much more; you will be relieving us of many little
embarrassments, which are sometimes worse than big
ones. (*A pause*)

TEISSIER

Have you seen Bourdon?

MARIE

No. Do we have to see Bourdon?

TEISSIER

You know well that this state of things can't last,
either for you or for me. Twelve thousand francs
that you want and twenty thousand you owe me
make thirty-two thousand francs that have come out
of my pocket. I am not risking anything, of course.
I know where to get back that money. But it certainly must come back to me. You won't be surprised to learn that I have taken steps toward that
end. Don't cry; don't cry. You have time enough
ahead of you to get sunken eyes and hollow cheeks.
Keep your twenty-year-old advantages; a little girl
of your age, blooming and flourishing, is unhappy
only when she wants to be. Understand me? Only
when she wants to be. (*He quits her suddenly, takes
his hat and goes over to Mrs. Vigneron*) Your second
daughter has just told me that you need twelve thousand francs. You need n't add anything to what she
said; it is n't necessary. Just you wait while I go
and get the money. (*He goes out abruptly*)

MRS. VIGNERON

Thanks, Marie dear. It makes one feel so silly and shamefaced to have to take money from that old codger! At the last minute I really came near deciding not to ask him for it.

MARIE

It's done.

MRS. VIGNERON

Judith — where are you going, child?

JUDITH

I'm going to leave you; I need sleep.

MRS. VIGNERON

Stay here, please do.

JUDITH

But, mama —

MRS. VIGNERON (*commandingly*)

Stay here! (*Judith obeys, and goes over to her mother*) Isn't our situation serious? Doesn't it interest you? We can't talk about it half enough.

JUDITH

What's the use talking about it? We are always saying over the same things without making the slightest decision. Don't you see it requires a different kind of woman than you to get us out of the scrape we are in?

MRS. VIGNERON

Soon you'll be saying that I am not doing my duty.

JUDITH

I don't say that. It isn't your fault that you don't understand anything about business.

MRS. VIGNERON

Then why don't you take charge of our business affairs?

JUDITH

Excuse me! I can't add a column of figures.

MRS. VIGNERON

Nobody is asking you to add a column of figures. We are asking you to be here, to take part in the discussion, and give us your opinion when you have any.

JUDITH

You know what my opinion is; and it won't change. We can't do anything, and there is nothing to do.

MRS. VIGNERON

But suppose they are robbing us?

JUDITH

Well, then they 'll rob us. You can't stop them and I can't. Neither can Marie. She ought to see plainly that we must wait for something to turn up. As for me, I should like a thousand times better — yes, a thousand times — to settle the whole thing to-day and take what they leave us, because they really *are* willing to leave us something. Then, when we no longer had to think about the past, we could think about the future.

MRS. VIGNERON

You talk very glibly about the future, Judith.

JUDITH

It worries me, but it does n't frighten me. I think Blanche is by far the most unfortunate of us. She is going to lose the man she loves.

MARIE

Nobody said she was going to lose him.

JUDITH

On the contrary, everybody says so. It 's as clear as daylight that Blanche won't be married. If I

were in her place, I should n't wait for Mr. de Saint-
Genis to ask for his release; I 'd throw him over
myself. •

MRS. VIGNERON

Now just see, Judith, what silly things you 've been
saying in the last five minutes. First you hurt me,
and now you have discouraged one of your sisters
and made the other one cry.

JUDITH (*going over to Blanche*)

Are you angry with me?

BLANCHE

No, I 'm not angry with you. You don't know Mr.
de Saint-Genis, or you would n't say such things. I
was very glad to be able to bring him a dowry, but
he won't love me less because I have lost it, and he
will have just the same desire to marry me. All the
trouble comes from his mother. But sooner or later
mothers have to give in, and Mrs. de Saint-Genis will
do just as the rest. She will find that the wisest
thing is to give her consent, when she sees that we
would marry without it. You are right, Judith,
when you say that we are not defending ourselves
very well. But though we may lack decision in dealing with our business affairs, I don't lack any in
regard to my marriage.

MRS. VIGNERON

Oh, dear! I don't understand you, girls. You are
always talking about decision: we lack decision; we
must have decision. You don't say anything else.
And when I propose some real idea, you are the first
ones to throw cold water on it. Come now, yes or
no: do you want me to dismiss Mr. Bourdon and get
another lawyer?

MARIE

Who?

MRS. VIGNERON

Who? The first one that comes along. (*To Judith*)
That man, for instance, who sent us his card.

JUDITH

Take him; I 'd just as lief.

MARIE

I 'm opposed to it.

MRS. VIGNERON

Well, children, I 'll have to settle it. If Mr. Bourdon
says one more word to me — just one more word —
that seems out of place to me, I 'll get rid of him and
send for this other man. But first of all, where is
this man's card? (*Silence*) Look in the desk for
it, Judith, and look carefully. Marie, you look on
the piano, perhaps it 's over there. Blanche, you
look, too. Do something! Look on the shelf over
the fireplace. (*Another silence*) You need n't look
any more, children. I have it in my pocket. (*To
Judith*) What are you laughing about?

JUDITH

I had to laugh. I was thinking that our enemies
know what they do with *their* things.

MRS. VIGNERON (*sadly*)

Are you going to begin again?

JUDITH

No; I 'm not going to, and I 'm sorry for what I
said. If I said anything wrong, I did n't mean to.
I wish this whole business was over with. It makes us
irritable and sour-tempered; and instead of fighting
our enemies we quarrel with one another. One might

think that we should have loved each other more
when we were happier; but the contrary is true.
(*She kisses her mother*)
[*Marie and Blanche make up. All are greatly
affected.*

ROSALIE (*entering*)
Mr. Bourdon, ma'am.

JUDITH
This time I *am* going.

MRS. VIGNERON
Go to bed, children. I 'll talk with Mr. Bourdon.
[*The three girls leave.*

BOURDON (*entering*)
Seeing how useless my previous advice proved, Mrs.
Vigneron, I had intended to let matters take their
course and not come to see you until you were ready
for me. Believe me, I have no hand in the bad news
I have been asked to bring you.

MRS. VIGNERON
I am beginning to get used to bad news, Mr.
Bourdon.

BOURDON
You must, madam, you must. In your position,
courage and resignation are of prime necessity.

MRS. VIGNERON
It strikes me, Mr. Bourdon, that my affairs give you
a good deal of trouble, considering the little you get
out of them. I have just heard of a man, very up-
right and intelligent, who will take charge of them.

BOURDON
Very well, madam, very well. Perhaps it would have
been a little more seemly to have saved me this visit

by letting me know of your decision earlier. Never mind. Shall I send all your papers here, or will they call at my office for them?

MRS. VIGNERON (*disconcerted*)

But I have n't made any arrangements with this man yet. Wait awhile; there 's no hurry.

BOURDON

On the contrary, madam, there is hurry. And since you have found, as you say, a capable, true and tried man, he should n't lose any time getting acquainted with the details of your estate — a matter of which he knows absolutely nothing. He is a business man, I suppose?

MRS. VIGNERON

Who told you he was a business man?

BOURDON

I guessed as much. Would it be indiscreet of me to ask who this man is? (*Mrs. Vigneron, after some hesitation, takes the card from her pocket and hands it to him; he returns it, smiling*) One last piece of advice, Mrs. Vigneron, which you may take or not, as you please. Duhamel, whose card this is, is an old lawyer who was debarred for embezzlement. Perhaps you do not know that in the legal profession black sheep are summarily expelled. After that setback, Duhamel set up a business office near the Court Buildings. It is n't my business to tell you what goes on in his office; but you will come to me with news about it before long.

MRS. VIGNERON

Tear up that card, Mr. Bourdon, and tell me what you came to see me about.

BOURDON

Mrs. Vigneron, you really deserve to be left in this man Duhamel's clutches. All he would have to do would be to come to an understanding with another scoundrel like himself — Lefort, for instance — and that would be the last of Mr. Vigneron's estate. You are angry with me because I spoil your illusions. Am I wrong to do so? Judge for yourself. In the face of your obstinate resolve to keep your real estate — a resolve I do not favor — I had to make an accurate survey of the situation. Well, in going over the bundle of mortgages, I found that one of them had fallen due. I wrote immediately to ask for a renewal. This request was refused. We need sixty-odd thousand francs to take up this mortgage, and we need it right now.

MRS. VIGNERON

What are we going to do?

BOURDON

That's what I am asking you. And that is n't all. Time is passing; are you ready to pay the inheritance taxes?

MRS. VIGNERON

But, Mr. Bourdon, according to you, our real estate is worth nothing; and where there is nothing, the authorities can't claim anything.

BOURDON

You are wrong. The authorities, in dealing with an estate, chase no wild geese. They collect taxes where they see the chance, regardless of who ought to be paying them.

MRS. VIGNERON

Are you sure of that?

BOURDON

What a question, Mrs. Vigneron! Why, my office
boy, a twelve-year-old boy, knows those things as
well as I do. Now you can just see what a hard time
we have with clients like you — entirely respectable,
of course, but also entirely ignorant. If by some
inadvertence we had not taken up this point together,
and then, later on — in going over the accounts after
the inevitable sale of your real estate — you had
found set down " Inheritance tax: so much," who
knows but you might have said: " Mr. Bourdon put
that money in his own pocket."

MRS. VIGNERON

Such an idea never would have occurred to me.

BOURDON

Well, Mrs. Vigneron, you are a little suspicious that
I am not fulfilling my duty toward you in all re-
spects; and that accusation is grave enough. But
let it go. While you are floundering about, doing
nothing, waiting for something or other to turn up,
that won't turn up, Teissier, like the business man he
is, has gone right ahead. He has put experts into
the factory. They have finished their report. In
short, Teissier has just sent me instructions to put
your factory up for sale.

MRS. VIGNERON

I don't believe you.

BOURDON

What, madam, you don't believe me? (*He takes a
letter from his pocket and hands it to her*) Teissier's
letter is clear enough; right to the point, just as he
always writes.

MRS. VIGNERON

Will you leave that letter with me, Mr. Bourdon?

BOURDON

I don't see what you could do with it, and it ought
to remain in my files.

MRS. VIGNERON

I'll return it to you to-morrow, if Mr. Teissier per-
sists in his determination.

BOURDON

As you please.

MRS. VIGNERON

You don't know, Mr. Bourdon, that our dealings with
Mr. Teissier have become very friendly.

BOURDON

Why should n't they be?

MRS. VIGNERON

He likes my daughters.

BOURDON

That 's fine, Mrs. Vigneron, that 's very fine.

MRS. VIGNERON

Why, he even took luncheon with us to-day.

BOURDON

I should be more surprised if you had taken luncheon
with him.

MRS. VIGNERON

Well, we have let Mr. Teissier know about our strait-
ened circumstances, and he has consented to lend us
a pretty round sum of money; and it is n't the first,
either.

BOURDON

Why do you ask Teissier for money?   Am I not here?
I told you, Mrs. Vigneron, that you could not look

to me for four or five hundred thousand francs for
imaginary building operations. Teissier would n't
let you have it either, I 'm dead sure of that. But
it is I, your lawyer, who ought to provide for your
everyday needs, and you would have pleased me if
you had not waited for me to tell you so.

MRS. VIGNERON

I beg your pardon, Mr. Bourdon; I did doubt you
for a moment. You must n't be angry with me; my
head is whirling in the midst of these complications;
and you were right when you said that I am ignorant.
If I could do as I wished, I would stay in my bed-
room and mourn for my husband; but what would
people say of a mother who did not defend her children as best she could? (*She sobs and throws herself
down on the couch*)

BOURDON (*going over to her, and speaking softly*)

I will try hard to get Teissier to put off the sale of
the factory, but on one condition: that you give up
your real estate. (*She looks at him fixedly*) You
certainly must understand why I suggest this condition, which is wholly to your advantage. I can't
think of spending useless energy and serving your
interests on one point only to have you getting me
in hot water on another. (*Silence*)

MRS. VIGNERON (*to Rosalie, who comes in*)

What is it, Rosalie?

ROSALIE

Mr. Merckens wishes to see you, ma'am.

MRS. VIGNERON (*rising*)

Very well. Show him in. (*To Bourdon*) Do you
mind having Mr. Merckens with you a moment, while
I talk this over with my daughters?

BOURDON

Go ahead, Mrs. Vigneron; go and talk it over with your daughters. (*She goes out at the left*)

MERCKENS (*entering*)

How d'ye do, Mr. Bourdon.

BOURDON

How are you, young man? How have you been since that unlucky dinner when I saw you last?

MERCKENS

The dinner was n't bad, but unfortunately we had to eat it on top of a rather nasty spectacle.

BOURDON

Right you are. Poor Vigneron was brought in right under our noses. . . .

MERCKENS

What did you have in mind when you took me to the restaurant that day?

BOURDON

That was your idea. You said to me, as we were coming out of the house: " I don't like the idea of going home with a white necktie and an empty stomach." I said: " Let 's dine somewhere, and then think up something to do during the rest of the evening." Well, we had a half-hearted meal, and the only thing we wanted to do was to go to bed. You see, people are always more sensitive to the death of others than they imagine, and it is particularly the case with a violent death. In spite of yourself you can't help thinking that the same thing might happen to you the very next day; and you don't feel much like laughing about it.

MERCKENS

Are you waiting to see Mrs. Vigneron?

BOURDON

> Yes. I ought not to wait, but Mrs. Vigneron is no
> ordinary client of mine, and I spoil her. You don't
> give lessons here any more, I suppose?

MERCKENS

> Miss Judith has n't taken any since her father died.

BOURDON

> If you 'll take my advice, you won't count on having
> her for a pupil any more, and you 'll look somewher
> else.

MERCKENS

> Why?

BOURDON

> I know what I 'm talking about. This family's new
> circumstances are going to force them to economize.

MERCKENS

> No?

BOURDON

> Yes.

MERCKENS

> Really?

BOURDON

> Really. (*A pause*)

MERCKENS

> But Mr. Vigneron was wealthy.

BOURDON

> He was n't wealthy; he made a lot of money, that 's
> all.

MERCKENS

> He did n't spend it on himself.

BOURDON

> He speculated with it, and that 's often worse.

MERCKENS

I thought that husky chap was going to leave his wife and children a fortune.

BOURDON

A fortune! You 'll do me a favor if you 'll show me where it is. Any minute, now, the Vigneron family are likely to find themselves in a bad predicament; and I can tell you, without shouting about my devotion to their interests, that they 'll owe it to me if they save a loaf of bread.

MERCKENS

Impossible!

BOURDON

That 's just where it stands, young man. Keep this news confidential, and make what use you can of it. (*A pause*)

MERCKENS (*in a low voice*)

What do they say about it here?

BOURDON

What would you expect them to say?

MERCKENS

These women can't be in very good spirits.

BOURDON

Well, what has happened to them has n't been any cause for rejoicing.

MERCKENS

Tears?

BOURDON

Tears!

MERCKENS (*going over to him with a smile*)

Do me a slight favor, will you? Be good enough to tell Mrs. Vigneron that I only had a minute to spare, that I did n't want to bother her, and that I 'll call again shortly.

BOURDON

You *will* call again?

MERCKENS

Not very likely.

BOURDON

Stay awhile, then, now that you are here, young man. You 'll be repaid in listening to the poor woman, and she 'll be thankful for a little kindness. She is really beginning to doubt whether anyone is interested in her misfortunes.

MERCKENS

It 's certain that Miss Judith won't continue with her lessons?

BOURDON

That 's very certain.

MERCKENS

You don't see anything ahead which could put Mrs. Vigneron and her daughters on their feet?

BOURDON

I do not.

MERCKENS

Then you bet I 'm off. That suits me better. No jabbering nonsense such as I could talk to Mrs. Vigneron would make her feel any better. I know myself too well. I should probably make some awful break; while you, with your great command of language, can find some excuse for me. How 's that?

BOURDON

Just as you say.

MERCKENS

Thanks. Good-bye, Mr. Bourdon.

BOURDON

Good-bye.

MERCKENS (*returning*)

Up to what time are you at your office?

BOURDON

Till seven o'clock.

MERCKENS

I 'm coming after you one of these days, and we 'll go to the theatre together. Is that all right?

BOURDON

Indeed it is.

MERCKENS

Which do you like best, grand opera or musical comedy?

BOURDON

Musical comedy.

MERCKENS

Musical comedy! You want something light. All right, we 'll see that kind of a show. Say, I hope this time we shan't have our evening spoiled by an apoplectic fit. So long!

BOURDON

So long, young man.

[*Merckens goes out at the rear while Mrs. Vigneron is coming in at the left.*

MRS. VIGNERON

Why did Mr. Merckens go away without waiting for me?

BOURDON

The young man was very much embarrassed, Mrs. Vigneron. When he saw me here, he understood that you were already occupied, and he thought best to postpone his visit until some more convenient time.

MRS. VIGNERON

He should n't have gone. I just told my daughters he was here, and they were going to entertain him.

BOURDON

Well, Mrs. Vigneron, what is the result of your conference with your daughters?

MRS. VIGNERON

Nothing, Mr. Bourdon.

BOURDON

What are you going to wait for now?

MRS. VIGNERON

We shan't do anything until we have seen Mr. Teissier.

BOURDON

And what do you expect he will say to you?

MRS. VIGNERON

There is no doubt about his intentions, that's true. He wants to sell our factory as much as he did yesterday. But this move would be so disastrous for us that he would n't dare to have a finger in it. We are going to have a straight talk with Mr. Teissier and we shan't hide the fact from him that he is n't treating us square.

BOURDON

Not square? That's rather strong talk. I doubt very much, Mrs. Vigneron, whether you can change his mind by using that kind of language to him.

MRS. VIGNERON

I'm not going to do the talking to Mr. Teissier. I lost my temper the first time, and I could easily do so again. Besides, considering the turn our affairs have taken, I would let them go as they please now, were it not for the fact that one of my daugh-

ters shows more perseverance than the rest of us —
her sisters and myself. Mr. Teissier really seems
to be well disposed toward her; so perhaps she can
succeed in making him change his mind.

BOURDON

Excuse me — you say Teissier has taken a liking
to one of your daughters?

MRS. VIGNERON

At least, we think so.

BOURDON

Which one?

MRS. VIGNERON

My second daughter, Marie.

BOURDON

And does Miss Marie reciprocate this kindly feeling
shown by Mr. Teissier?

MRS. VIGNERON

What in the world are you thinking about, Mr.
Bourdon. You're not figuring on making a match,
are you?

BOURDON

Wait a minute, Mrs. Vigneron. If Teissier were disposed to marry this young lady, she would n't do a
bad stroke of business in accepting him; but I had
something else in mind. You know Teissier is no
longer young; he has reached an age where the
slightest sickness might carry him off. If this very
sudden affection he is showing toward your daughter
should lead him, later on, to make some provisions
for her, perhaps it would be just as well if you
did n't antagonize the old man at this point.

MRS. VIGNERON

We expect nothing from Mr. Teissier. Let him live
as long as he can and do what he pleases with his
money. But this factory he wants to sell belongs
to both of us, and not to him alone. To do as he
pleases with my husband's work and my children's
property would be to abuse the rights given him by
the law.

BOURDON

I won't argue further.

ROSALIE (*entering*)

Mr. Teissier is here, ma'am.

MRS. VIGNERON

Just a minute, Rosalie. (*To Bourdon*) Is it necessary for you to meet?

BOURDON

Yes; I should prefer it. Please understand perfectly, Mrs. Vigneron, that I am working for Teissier
as well as you. I make no difference between you.
All I want is for you to come to some decision, so
that I may know what to do.

MRS. VIGNERON

Very well. I'll send my daughter in. (*She goes out
at the left, gesturing to Rosalie to have Teissier come
in*)

[*Teissier enters.*

BOURDON

You here — you?

TEISSIER

Yes, I'm here.

BOURDON

What's this I've been hearing? Nobody sees you
anywhere else but here.

TEISSIER

I have been here several times. What of it?

BOURDON

You are hostile to the interests of this family, and yet you sit at their table?

TEISSIER

What are you kicking about, as long as what I do does n't interfere with you?

BOURDON

My position is n't an easy one as it is. You are making it more difficult.

TEISSIER

Go right ahead as we agreed, Bourdon — do you understand? Don't bother yourself about my doings.

BOURDON

Miss Marie will get what she wants out of you.

TEISSIER

Miss Marie will get nothing.

BOURDON

It seems you have a weakness for this young lady.

TEISSIER

Who told you so?

BOURDON

Her mother.

TEISSIER

What is she meddling for?

BOURDON

You had better get ready for a carefully planned siege on the part of your simple maiden. I warn you they are looking to her to bring you to terms.

TEISSIER

Take your hat, Bourdon, and go back to your office.

BOURDON

All right; just as you say. (*Returning to Teissier*) I need n't wait any longer, eh? Shall I start the thing going?

TEISSIER

Sure! (*Calling Bourdon back*) Listen, Bourdon! I told you about my talk with Lefort, did n't I? He 's an ugly customer, and he 's right after us. The wise thing will be to go easy with him, don't you think? He is still in charge of the building operations.

BOURDON

What? Have you had dealings with Lefort, after that wretched scene when he insulted both of us?

TEISSIER

Still thinking about that, are you? If we should refuse to see people just because a few strong words had passed between us, then we could n't see anybody at all.

BOURDON

Well, it 's your business, after all. I don't know why I should mix into it. I promised you should get the real estate, and you shall. The rest does n't worry me. (*Marie enters; he goes over to her and speaks in a low tone*) I leave you with Teissier, my dear young lady. Try to convince him; a woman sometimes succeeds where we fail. If you get anything out of him, you will be more fortunate and cleverer than I am. (*He goes out*)

TEISSIER

Here is the money you asked me for. You told me it was intended for your tradespeople. Meet them

yourself. Look sharp at the bills they render; don't
be afraid to beat them down as much as you can; and,
above all, take good care not to pay the same bill
twice. (*Detaining her*) Where is my receipt?

MARIE

I 'll give it to you by and by.

TEISSIER

I ought to take it in one hand while I am handing
over the money with the other. Just this minute I
am flustered. (*She goes to the writing-desk and puts
the banknotes in a drawer; then she comes back.
There is a moment of silence*) You have something
to tell me, and I have something to tell you, too.
Come sit beside me, won't you, and have a nice
friendly talk. (*They sit down*) What do you figure
on doing?

MARIE

I don't understand your question.

TEISSIER

My question is simple enough, nevertheless. I told
you before that there would be fifty thousand francs
coming to you; no more. You can't think of holding on to this apartment and keeping open house
until your last cent is gone. What do you figure
on doing?

MARIE

A relative of my mother's who lives in the country
has invited us to come and settle near him.

TEISSIER

Your mother's relative is like all relatives. He made
that suggestion thinking to get an invitation in return; he won't cling to the idea when it will be his
turn to carry out the suggestion.

MARIE

Then we 'll stay in Paris.

TEISSIER

What are you going to do in Paris?

MARIE

My oldest sister is ready to give music lessons, when the time comes.

TEISSIER

Good. Your oldest sister, if she carries out that idea, will promptly let the rest of the family support themselves. She will want her money herself, and she will be right.

MARIE

But I count on getting something to do, too.

TEISSIER

What?

MARIE

That 's it, what? I don't know yet. It 's so hard for a woman to find work, and she gets so little for it.

TEISSIER

That brings us to what I wanted to say. (*A pause; he continues with some hesitation and embarrassment*) I know of a house where, if you want to, you can come to live. You will get your room and board there, and every month a small sum which you can save up for a rainy day. You will not have to look any further for a place.

MARIE

Whose house? Yours?

TEISSIER (*with an equivocal half-smile*)
Mine.

MARIE (*after a display of emotion; not knowing how she ought to interpret his words, nor how she ought to reply*) What you propose is impossible. In the first place, my mother would not let me leave her.

TEISSIER

Yes; I had an idea your mother might interpose some opposition. But you are of age now and can consider your best interests without consulting anybody.

MARIE

I told you no, Mr. Teissier; *no!*

TEISSIER

Would n't you be mighty glad to let your family stay in the ditch and go out and do something on your own account? That 's the way I should feel, if I were in your place.

MARIE

That is n't the way I feel.

TEISSIER

What good do you see in all scrambling around together, instead of going your separate ways?

MARIE

Just the advantage of not being separated. (*Leaving him*) Sometimes it is good to have consolation nearby. That way you are not troubled so much with certain sudden events that would otherwise be disconcerting. (*A pause*)

TEISSIER

It is some time now since I began coming here. I don't stay away from my business without a good reason. You are n't stupid — you have a quick wit. You ought to be able to see through it.

MARIE

I was thinking of something else.

TEISSIER

What?

MARIE

I was thinking only of my family. I can think only of the fate that awaits them, now that they have lost everything.

TEISSIER (*with a smile*)

So you are trying to get the best of me and worm something out of me for them?

MARIE

Oh, Mr. Teissier! I have enough sorrow without your adding anything to it. You want to know what I thought; I will tell you. I was thinking that you are no longer young, that you live a very dreary and lonely life, that you have no children, and so you like the company of other people — those were my thoughts. Yet you were right, I admit. We did not have you coming here before my father died; and we should n't have begun afterward. We shall have to take things as they come, meeting our difficulties courageously, and telling ourselves that after all women are never unhappy when they love each other, and are brave, and stand by one another. (*A pause*)

TEISSIER

How many are there of you? You, your mother and your two sisters?

MARIE

And Rosalie.

TEISSIER

Where does Rosalie come in?

MARIE

She is a saint. She brought us all up.

TEISSIER

What do you do to keep your servants? I could never get one attached to me. There are four of you — Rosalie does n't count. Unfortunately, four is too many; you can understand that. Even to please a little friend I want to have with me, I can't be responsible for a whole family. They would bore me to death.

MARIE

Nobody asked you to; and nobody dreamed of such a thing.

TEISSIER

I did n't want to tell you, but you guessed it. A fellow does n't complain of being alone as long as he is young; but at my age it is tiresome and unsafe.

MARIE

If you are alone, it 's because you prefer to be.

TEISSIER

I ought to get married?

MARIE

It is n't necessary to get married to have people around you. You still have your parents.

TEISSIER

I don't see them any more, because I wanted to get out of reach of their demands for money; they are starving. I want very much to get hold of a little woman of simple tastes, kind and trustworthy, who will conduct herself decently in my house, and who won't steal everything in sight. Perhaps later on I 'll see whether I ought to marry her. But you women are all lambs before marriage, and God knows what afterward. I would regulate my conduct according to hers; she would not be badly off while I was living, and she 'd have no cause to complain after I died. Married or not, it would be just the same for her.

MARIE

Take your hat, Mr. Teissier, and go away. I don't want to have you near me another minute. I believe you are unhappy, and I pity you. I believe your proposal was an honest and proper one, and I thank you for it. But it could have another meaning, a meaning so loathsome that my heart trembles at the very thought of it. Go away.

TEISSIER (*standing, embarrassed, blubbering*)

Just stop and think of what you are saying to me.

MARIE

No more! Not a word! I ought to be ashamed of having spoken to you about my family; I ought to be ashamed for them as well as for myself. Think it over. Consider what kind of a man my father was, and what you owe to his honesty, to his work, to his memory. (*She goes hurriedly to the desk, takes out the banknotes and hands them back to him*) Take your money. Don't be embarrassed; take it. Mr. Bourdon has just offered to help us, and we shall get from him what we could not have asked of you. Go now! Go, before I call Rosalie to show you out. (*A pause; Rosalie enters*) Here she is now. What is it, Rosalie?

ROSALIE

Mrs. de Saint-Genis is here.

MARIE

Very well, show her in.

ROSALIE

What's the matter, dearie; you are blushing? (*Looking alternately from Marie to Teissier*) I hope nobody has said anything to you they should n't?

MARIE

Show Mrs. de Saint-Genis in.

TEISSIER

I 'll go. I 'll stop in and see Bourdon on my way,
as to whether there is still a way to fix things up;
but don't count too much on it. Good-bye!

ROSALIE

It is n't wise to leave such a child with a man of
his age!

[*Mrs. de Saint-Genis, entering, encounters Teissier
on his way out.*

MRS. DE SAINT-GENIS

How do you do, Miss Vigneron. I never come here
these days without meeting Mr. Teissier. Is that a
good sign? Are you going to come to terms with
him?

MARIE

No, Mrs. de Saint-Genis.

MRS. DE SAINT-GENIS

Pshaw! I thought you were.

MARIE

Why?

MRS. DE SAINT-GENIS

An old man ought to find it pleasant to be in a house
like yours.

MARIE

Mr. Teissier came to-day for the last time.

MRS. DE SAINT-GENIS

Then I can sincerely say I am sorry for you. Is
your sister at home?

MARIE

Yes.

MRS. DE SAINT-GENIS

Please have her come here. Don't bother your
mother; it is n't necessary; I can see her another
time. I want to talk with Blanche.

MARIE

She 'll be right in. (*Goes out*)

MRS. DE SAINT-GENIS

It is decidedly better to have a talk with this young
woman and tell her straight out that the marriage is
not postponed, but broken off. It is better for her
to know where she stands, and it will clear my own
mind, too. For the first time in his life George was
going contrary to my wishes. He clung to his sweetheart, and wanted to marry her. Fortunately another good match came along, and I gave him his
choice — to obey me or never see me again. He gave
in. But what a brigand a young man twenty-three
years old can be! And as for this giddy miss, who
could n't wait until she was married — well, so much
the worse for her.

BLANCHE (*entering*)

Oh, I am so glad to see you, Mrs. de Saint-Genis!

MRS. DE SAINT-GENIS

How do you do, child; how do you do.

BLANCHE

Give me a good hug!

MRS. DE SAINT-GENIS

Of course I will.

BLANCHE

You know I love you so much.

MRS. DE SAINT-GENIS

Come, Blanche, dear, don't get so excited. I have
come to-day to talk seriously with you; so listen to

me like the great big woman you are. It is time, at
your age, to use a little reason. (*She sits down*)
My son loves you, child; I tell you very frankly,
he loves you a great deal. Don't interrupt me. I
know, too, that you feel somewhat the same toward
him — a light, thoughtless affection such as young
girls often have when they meet a nice young man.

BLANCHE

Oh, Mrs. de Saint-Genis, you are disparaging a feeling which goes very much deeper than that.

MRS. DE SAINT-GENIS

Well, I was wrong, then. Love is a very fine thing,
very vague and poetic; but a passion, however great
it may be, never lasts very long, and never gets anywhere. I know what I am talking about. You can't
pay the rent and the baker's bill with that kind of
currency. You know I am not rich; my son's position is not yet assured; and certain deplorable circumstances have endangered your domestic situation,
and perhaps will ruin you. Now, my child, I want
to ask you if under these circumstances it would be
very discreet to go on with a marriage which promises
so unfavorably?

BLANCHE (*quickly*)

We ought to be married, Mrs. de Saint-Genis, and
we are going to be.

MRS. DE SAINT-GENIS (*sweetly*)

You are, if I say so.

BLANCHE

You will give your consent.

MRS. DE SAINT-GENIS

I don't think so.

BLANCHE

Yes, Mrs. de Saint-Genis; yes, you will! There are affections so sincere that even a mother has no right to come between them. There are promises so sacred that a man is dishonored if he does not fulfil them.

MRS. DE SAINT-GENIS

What promises are you talking about? (*Silence*) I admit, if that suits you, that a marriage was planned between you and my son; but it was subject to certain conditions, and it is not my fault if you cannot live up to them. I was hoping, child, you would think of that yourself. I was hoping you would bow in submission before a changed situation which is nobody's fault, but which necessarily alters the expectations of you both.

BLANCHE

George does not talk that way, Mrs. de Saint-Genis. His expectations are the same as ever. The loss of our money has n't affected him in the least bit, and I think he is only more eager to marry me.

MRS. DE SAINT-GENIS

Leave my son out of the matter, won't you? I tell him every day he is too young yet to know what he does or says.

BLANCHE

George is twenty-three.

MRS. DE SAINT-GENIS

Twenty-three! Indeed!

BLANCHE

At that age, Mrs. de Saint-Genis, a man has passions, and will-power, and certain rights.

MRS. DE SAINT-GENIS

You insist on talking about my son — very well,
we 'll talk about him. Are you so sure of his feelings? I don't see them in the same light as you.
Placed, as he is, between an affection which is dear
to him and a future in which he is interested, the
poor boy is uncertain, hesitating.

BLANCHE (*rising suddenly*)

You are deceiving me, Mrs. de Saint-Genis.

MRS. DE SAINT-GENIS

No, child, I am not deceiving you — no, indeed! I
have given my son the benefit of my serious reflection,
and I should be sorry for him if he did not make
good use of it. Another thing: do we ever know
what is going on in a man's brain? George is no
more sincere than the next man. Perhaps he is only
waiting for my order to get out of an embarrassing
situation.

BLANCHE

Well, give him that order.

MRS. DE SAINT-GENIS

He would obey it.

BLANCHE

No, Mrs. de Saint-Genis.

MRS. DE SAINT-GENIS

I assure you he would, even if reluctantly.

BLANCHE

If it comes to that, Mrs. de Saint-Genis, your son
would decide to confess to you something he has
withheld out of respect for me.

MRS. DE SAINT-GENIS

What confession? (*Silence*) So! I thought you
would be the first one to break the reserve on that

subject. You may spare yourself any delicate confidence. I know all about it. (*Blanche, confused
and blushing, runs to Mrs. de Saint-Genis and throws
herself at her feet, with her head on the older woman's
knees; Mrs. de Saint-Genis rebukes her, caressing her
all the while*) I don't care to inquire, child, whether
you or George was responsible. It is your mother
and I who are at fault, for leaving you two children
together when you should have been watched. You
see, I do not attach any undue importance to the
result of a moment of forgetfulness, justified by your
youth, and all the surrounding circumstances. You
ought to want your fault to remain a secret; my son
is an honorable man who would never betray you.
So much said, the next question is: is it necessary
for both of you to sacrifice your whole lives for the
sake of a slip? Would n't it be better to forget it?

BLANCHE (*rising*)

Never. (*A pause*)

MRS. DE SAINT-GENIS (*she has risen, and her tone
changes*) You will not be surprised, Blanche, if my
son does n't come here any more.

BLANCHE

I want to hear that from *him*.

MRS. DE SAINT-GENIS

Are you hoping he will disobey his mother?

BLANCHE

Yes; to do his duty.

MRS. DE SAINT-GENIS

You should not have forgotten yours, in the first
place.

BLANCHE

Go ahead, wound me, humiliate me; I know I deserve it.

MRS. DE SAINT-GENIS

I feel more like pitying you, Blanche, than hurting you. But it seems to me that a young girl, after a misfortune like yours, should bow her head and submit.

BLANCHE

You shall see, Mrs. de Saint-Genis, what a young girl can do toward getting the reparation due her.

MRS. DE SAINT-GENIS

Well, what will you do?

BLANCHE

I 'll find out first whether your son has two kinds of talk, one for you and another for me. I don't say yet that he has. He knows what you want, and so he conceals his own thoughts from you. But if I am dealing with a coward who hides behind his mother's skirts, he need n't think he can get rid of me so easily. Everywhere, everywhere he goes, I shall injure him. I 'll ruin his standing, and spoil his future.

MRS. DE SAINT-GENIS

You 'll get yourself talked about that way; that 's all. Perhaps that 's what you want to do. Fortunately, your mother will stop that. She 'll think a stain on the family's name is enough without adding a scandal to it. Good day, Blanche.

BLANCHE (*holding her*)

Don't go, Mrs. de Saint-Genis.

MRS. DE SAINT-GENIS (*sweetly*)

We have nothing more to say.

BLANCHE

Stay here. See, I am weeping! I am suffering!
Feel my hand; I am burning up with fever.

MRS. DE SAINT-GENIS

Yes; I understand the frame of mind you are in;
but that will pass. Whereas, if you should be married to my son, your regrets and his would last
forever.

BLANCHE

We love each other.

MRS. DE SAINT-GENIS

To-day, yes — but to-morrow?

BLANCHE

Give us your consent, I implore you.

MRS. DE SAINT-GENIS

Must I repeat that word you just said to me?
Never!

[*Blanche leaves her and walks back and forth across
the stage in a state of great emotion and violent
grief; then she drops into an armchair.*

MRS. DE SAINT-GENIS (*going up to Blanche*)

I am very sorry, child, to seem so cruel and to leave
you in this condition. But I am right; absolutely
right. A woman of my age and experience, who has
seen all there is to see in this world, knows the true
value of things and does n't exaggerate one thing at
the expense of another.

BLANCHE (*throwing herself on her knees*)

Listen, Mrs. de Saint-Genis. What will become of
me if your son does not marry me? It is his duty.
There is nothing nobler or kinder in a man than to
cling to the woman he loves. Believe me, if it were

an ordinary engagement, I should n't humiliate myself to the extent of holding him back. Yes, I should
break my heart rather than offer it to one who dis-
dained it, or was unworthy of it. But your son must
marry me; I say again it is his duty. Everything
gives way before that fact. You speak about the
future. The future will be as he pleases. I am
thinking only of the past. I should die of shame and
sorrow.

MRS. DE SAINT-GENIS

Child that you are, to speak of dying at your age!
Come, get up and listen to me now. I see that you
really do love my son more than I thought, if you
still cling to a boy who is almost poverty-stricken.
But if I should consent to this marriage, in a year
— yes, in six months, you would bitterly reproach
me for my weakness. Love would pass, but you
would have a household still. What do you think
would be your lot then? Shabby, worried, vulgar,
nursing your children yourself, while your discontented husband would be reproaching you all the time
on account of the sacrifice he had made for you.
Do what I ask. Make the sacrifice yourself instead.
Can't you see how different all will be then? George
will not have abandoned you; it will be you who have
dismissed him generously. He will be under obliga-
tion to you. You will hold forever a place way down
deep in his heart. Men always remain sensitive to
the memory of a woman they have truly loved, even
for an hour. It is so rare! And what will happen
to you after that? I 'll tell you. Little by little the
love for my son, which seems so tremendous to you
just now, will disappear. Yes; quicker than you

think. You are young, pretty, full of charm for
young men. Ten, yes, twenty, young fellows will
come along. You will choose, not the most attractive,
but the one who is best off. And on your wedding
day you will think of me and say to yourself: " Mrs.
de Saint-Genis was right."

BLANCHE

What kind of woman are you, Mrs. de Saint-Genis,
to give me such advice as that? What would your
son say if he knew it? I would rather be his mistress than the wife of another man.

MRS. DE SAINT-GENIS

His mistress! Pretty words to come from you! My
son shall know what you have just said. It's one
more sign of your waywardness.

BLANCHE

No, no, Mrs. de Saint-Genis; don't repeat that
awful word. I blushed when I said it.

MRS. DE SAINT-GENIS

His mistress! Evidently you can stand anything;
so I am going to tell you all. I should never have
broken off your marriage for a matter of dollars
and cents. But I want my son to have a wife whose
past is above suspicion, and who will give him no
anxiety for the future. (*She goes toward the door*)

BLANCHE

Oh, oh, oh! You insult me, Mrs. de Saint-Genis,
without any reason — without pity!

MRS. DE SAINT-GENIS

Let me go, young woman. His mistress! Why,
that's the talk of a fallen woman! (*She repulses
Blanche gently and goes out*)

BLANCHE

A fallen woman! She dares to call me — Oh, God!
(*She bursts into tears*) Oh, it's all over now! George
is weak, his mother controls him . . . he will obey
her. A fallen woman! (*She weeps increasingly*)
A fine fellow like him! Not at all like that woman!
And yet under her thumb! . . . I can't stand it.
A little while ago my hands were burning hot; now
they are cold as ice. (*She rings and comes to the
front of the stage; she speaks in a broken voice*)
He is young . . . barely twenty-three . . . gentle,
refined, charming . . . some other woman will love
him and marry him.

ROSALIE (*entering*)

Is it you, dearie, who rang for me?

BLANCHE (*going to her sadly*)

I'm cold, nursey. Throw something over me.

ROSALIE (*having scrutinized her*)

I'm going to put you to bed; that'll be much better.

BLANCHE

No.

ROSALIE

Do as I tell you, if you don't want to be sick.

BLANCHE

Oh, yes; I am going to be sick.

ROSALIE

Come, Rosalie is going to undress you. It won't be
the first time.

BLANCHE

Call mama.

ROSALIE

You don't need your mother; I'm here.

BLANCHE

I'm not going to be married, Rosalie.

ROSALIE

Well, it's an ill wind that blows no good! We've spoiled you; but not enough to make you prefer that she-devil and her monkey. That's what they are. That marriage, I tell you, wasn't the right kind for you. If they had listened to your father and me, it wouldn't have been considered a minute.

BLANCHE (*out of her head*)

My father! I see my father now! He's reaching out his arms to me and beckoning me to come with him.

ROSALIE

Come and lie down, Blanchy.

BLANCHE

Your Blanchy is a fallen woman! You didn't know it. I'm a fallen woman!

ROSALIE

Don't talk that way, dearie; it isn't nice. Come, come with your old nursey.

BLANCHE

Oh, I can't bear it! (*She cries out*) Marie! Marie! Marie! (*She grows weak in Rosalie's arms and slips little by little to the floor*)

MARIE (*entering and throwing herself down by her sister*) Blanche! Blanche!

ROSALIE

Keep still, girlie; it's no use, she can't hear. Take her up gently, poor lamb, and we'll put her to bed.

BLANCHE (*murmuring*)

Fallen woman!

MRS. VIGNERON (*appearing*)

What 's the matter? (*She throws herself down by Blanche*)

ROSALIE

Come away from her, ma'am; you 'll bother us more than you 'll help. (*Judith appears*)

MRS. VIGNERON

Judith, come here. (*They walk aside together*) You were right, Judith. We 've got nothing in the world. They 're putting your sister to bed; to-morrow it will be your turn, and the next day mine. You still think the best way is to settle everything?

JUDITH

Yes; I still think so.

MRS. VIGNERON

Good. Take Rosalie with you and go to see Mr. Bourdon. Tell him I accept everything, approve everything, and all I want now is to have it over with. You can add that we are just as much in a hurry as he is. That 's your idea, too?

JUDITH

That 's my idea.

MRS. VIGNERON

Go ahead then. (*They separate*) I should like to keep what belongs to me; but the first thing is to save my children.

CURTAIN

THE FOURTH ACT

*A cheaply furnished dining-room, with a shabby-gen-
teel look. Here and there a few chairs; in one place
everything is reminiscent of the furniture of the previous acts, and plainly not fitting these new surround-
ings. There are two single doors, one at the left and the
other at the back. At the rear, to the right, a mahogany
table covered with red oilcloth stands against the wall;
on this table appears a loaf of bread; also cups and
other dishes.*

ROSALIE

Come in, Mr. Merckens. They 'll be glad to see
somebody they know.

MERCKENS (*having looked about him*)

Well, well! The lawyer was n't lying to me. This
is poverty, sure enough!

ROSALIE

You 're looking at our new home? Yes, it is n't very
much! Oh, Lord; yesterday and to-day are two
different things.

MERCKENS

What 's happened to the family?

ROSALIE

Ruined, Mr. Merckens. My poor missus and the
girls have lost everything. I 'm not saying how it
happened, but I 've got my opinion, and I 'll keep it,

too.   You see, when business men get into a house
where a person has just died, you may as well say:
" Here come the vultures."   They don't leave anything they can carry away.

MERCKENS

It is n't a pleasant place any more, eh, Rosalie?

ROSALIE

Not for anybody, Mr. Merckens, not for anybody.

MERCKENS

Why don't you find another place?

ROSALIE

How can the girls get along without me, any more
than I can without them?   I 'm one more mouth to
be fed, true enough; but you bet I earn what I eat.
You must n't think you can stay to luncheon with
us, Mr. Merckens.   In the old days, when I saw you
coming at this hour, I did n't need any orders to
know what to do; you 'd find your place ready at
the table; but things are different now.   I 'll go and
tell Mrs. Vigneron you are here.

MERCKENS

No; don't bother Mrs. Vigneron.   Just tell Miss
Judith I am here.
[*Judith enters.*

ROSALIE

Here she is now.

JUDITH

How do you do, Mr. Merckens.
[*Merckens bows.*

ROSALIE

But of course, if a good cup of coffee will do you,
we can still offer you that.

JUDITH

Leave us, Rosalie —
[*Rosalie goes out.*

JUDITH (*to Merckens*)

First of all, I 've a little bone to pick with you, and
then that 'll be out of the way. I wrote to you
twice asking you to come and see me. Once ought
to be enough.

MERCKENS (*awkwardly*)

Are you sure you wrote me twice?

JUDITH

You know well I did.

MERCKENS

No, really; your first letter did n't reach me.

JUDITH

Well, never mind. I don't need to tell you the conditions we are reduced to; you saw the moment you
came in.

MERCKENS (*half serious, half joking*)

Tell me about it.

JUDITH

It 's a story you would n't be interested in, and it
would n't be pleasant for me to tell. In a word, we
did n't have money enough to fight for our rights;
we had to have a hundred thousand francs in cash.

MERCKENS

Why did n't you tell me? I would have found the
money.

JUDITH

It 's too late now. Please sit down. Mr. Merckens,
you have seen, and you remember, our family life.
We were very happy; very fond of one another; we

knew very few people outside, and cared to know
none. We did n't think that some day we should
have need of acquaintances, and that then we
should n't have any. (*Merckens looks at his watch*)
Are you in a hurry?

MERCKENS

Yes; I am. Will you please cut the story short?
You wanted to see me; here I am. You want to
ask me something. What is it? Perhaps it would
be just as well for me to tell you that I am not a
very obliging person.

JUDITH

Shall I go on?

MERCKENS

Yes, certainly; go ahead.

JUDITH

Here is what I first thought of; I 'll start with the
simplest and surest thing. I am thinking of turning
to account the fine lessons you have given me, by
giving lessons myself.

MERCKENS (*touching her knee*)

What, poor child — you 've got down to that?

JUDITH

Come, come, Mr. Merckens; please call me " Miss,"
as you have been used to do, and answer me seriously.

MERCKENS

Lessons! In the first place, are you capable of giving lessons? I 'm not so sure of it. But let 's suppose you are. Would you do what is necessary to
get pupils? To get them, you have to play the part
of a beggar. You don't get any by being dignified
and putting on airs. But it is possible that people
might take pity on you, and in four or five years

— not before — you might have enough pupils.
Your pupils would as often as not be disagreeable;
their parents would nearly always be brutes. What
is a poor little music teacher to a lot of philistines
that don't even know what C major is? You need n't
look any farther, for instance, than your dad . . .

JUDITH

We won't speak of my father.

MERCKENS

Surely a fellow can laugh a little — he did n't leave
you anything. (*A pause*)

JUDITH

Let 's put aside the question of music lessons a
minute; we can come back to that. Now in what
I am going to say to you, Mr. Merckens, please
don't think I am prompted by vanity or presump-
tion; I am just trying to make use of what talent
I have for music. I have composed a good deal;
you know that. With the little things I 've already
written, and others I can produce, can't I get a living for my family?

MERCKENS (*after laughing*)

Look at me. (*He laughs again*) Never, never say
that again; understand? I mean what you have
just said to me. You 'd be the laughing-stock of the
whole world. (*He laughs again*) Earn a living!
Is that all?

JUDITH

No, it is n't. We were talking once about a profession that did n't strike me favorably then, and still
does n't more than half appeal to me. But the way
my family is fixed, I ought not to hesitate at anything to help them out. The stage?

MERCKENS

Too late.

JUDITH

Why can't I do as others have — women who felt
undecided at first, but summoned up their courage
and went into it?

MERCKENS

Too late.

JUDITH

Perhaps I have natural qualities — and lack only
work and experience?

MERCKENS

Too late. It's no use thinking of the stage without
preparing for it a long time. You'll never be an
artist. It isn't in you. As you are now, all you'd
find on the stage would be disillusionment . . . or
adventures; and that isn't what you are after, is it?

JUDITH

But what can I do, then?

MERCKENS

Nothing. I see the fix you are in. You're not the
first one I've seen in the same situation, and made
the same reply to. There are no resources for a
woman; or, at least, only one. Now I'll tell you
the whole truth in one sentence. If you are good,
people will respect you without doing anything for
you; and if you're not, they'll do things for you
without respecting you. There's no other way
about it. Are you going to take up the subject
of giving lessons again?

JUDITH

It's no use. I'm sorry to have bothered you.

MERCKENS

You want me to go?

JUDITH

I shan't stop you.

MERCKENS

Good-bye, Miss Judith.

JUDITH

Good-bye, Mr. Merckens.

MERCKENS (*at the door*)

There was nothing else to tell her.

MARIE (*entering*)

Well?

JUDITH

Well, if Mr. Merckens is right, and if things are as he says, we are n't out of our difficulties yet. Meanwhile, here are all my plans upset; those you know of, and another one I had kept to myself.

MARIE

What other?

JUDITH

What 's the use telling you?

MARIE

Tell me, anyway.

JUDITH

I did think, for a while, of making use of my voice, by going on the stage.

MARIE

You, sister, on the stage!

JUDITH

Well, why not? We must be doing something, and we 've got to take what comes. We can't wait till we have got down to our last cent. Mama is n't able to go to work, and furthermore we don't want her to.

Who knows whether poor Blanche will ever recover
her reason? Well, then, there's just you and me;
and what is there you can do, dearie? You would
have to work twelve hours a day to earn a franc and
a half.

MARIE

Tell me, really and truly, what you think of Blanche's
condition? How do you find her?

JUDITH

One day better and the next day worse. We expect
her to recognize us any moment; but as yet she
does n't seem to see anyone or hear anything. I 've
been thinking over this misfortune; and perhaps we
have escaped a worse one. If Blanche, in that condition, had heard of the marriage of Mr. de Saint-
Genis, might it not have killed her? She is alive.
That 's the main thing. We have her still with us.
If we must always take care of her, we will. If we
must go hungry for her, we 'll do that, too. She
is n't our sister now — she 's our little girl.

MARIE

How good you are, sister; I love you so much!
(*They embrace*)

JUDITH

I love you, too. At times I am blunt; but I always
have you here, in my heart. It seems to me that I,
the eldest sister — " big sister," as you call me —
I am the one who should find a way out of our
troubles. I don't know how to do it. I 've looked,
and I can't find a way. If the only thing needed were
to go through fire and water for the rest of you, I
should have done that before now. (*A pause*)

MARIE

Has mama said anything about a visit from Mr.
Bourdon?

JUDITH

No. What was he doing here?

MARIE

Mr. Teissier sent him to ask me to be his wife.

JUDITH

I 'm not surprised. It was easy enough to see that
Mr. Teissier took a liking to you, and sooner or later
the idea of marriage was bound to come to him.

MARIE

Would you advise me to accept him?

JUDITH

You must n't ask my advice on that point. You are
the one concerned; it is for you to decide. Think
it over well, look at it from all sides, but by all means
think only of yourself. If you are frightened at our
situation, and you look back regretfully to the times
when we had plenty of money, marry Mr. Teissier.
He will make you pay dearly enough for your comfort and security. But if I understand you, and
the way you love your mother and sisters, and how
you could do for them what would be repulsive if
you alone were concerned, we should be very wrong
— all the guiltier — to advise you to make the greatest sacrifice a woman can make.

MARIE

What you say is right from the heart; kiss me
again.

[*Rosalie enters at the rear; in one hand she carries
a coffee-pot, in the other a casserole full of milk;
she places them on the table, and then draws near*

*the two sisters and watches them, sighing; Marie
and Judith separate.*

JUDITH

Is luncheon ready?

ROSALIE

Yes, miss. I 'll serve it whenever you wish.

MARIE

Judith is going to help you with the table, Rosalie.
[*Judith and Rosalie carry the table to the front of
the stage, placing it at the right; Rosalie arranges
the cups and serves the coffee while Judith places the
chairs. Marie, meanwhile, goes to the door at the
left and opens it. Blanche comes in, followed by her
mother. Blanche is pale, limp, and stares stupidly,
her attitude being that of a harmless insane person.
Mrs. Vigneron is aged and whitened. Marie helps
Blanche to a place, and then they sit down one by
one, except Rosalie, who takes her coffee standing.
There is a prolonged silence, and an atmosphere of
utter desolation.*

MRS. VIGNERON (*suddenly bursting out*)

Oh, children; if your father could see us! (*Tears
and sobbing*)
[*At that moment Bourdon steps quietly into the
room.*

ROSALIE (*to Bourdon*)

How did you get in?

BOURDON

By the open door. You ought not leave your outside door open. Thieves could steal everything
you 've got.

ROSALIE (*speaking directly at him*)

No fear of that. That job has been done — and done brown.

BOURDON (*to Mrs. Vigneron, who has risen*)

Don't let me disturb you, madam; I 'll wait until you have finished luncheon.

MRS. VIGNERON (*going to him*)

What have you got to say to me, Mr. Bourdon?

BOURDON (*in a low tone*)

This time, madam, I 've come for Teissier, regarding a matter very dear to him. I assume you have let your daughter know about the offer I spoke about?

MRS. VIGNERON

Certainly.

BOURDON

Do I have your permission to renew the offer to her, in your presence?

MRS. VIGNERON

Very well, you have my consent. Judith, dear, take your sister away. Marie, Mr. Bourdon wishes to speak with us.

[*Judith leads Blanche out.*

BOURDON (*to Marie*)

Your mother has told you, young lady, of the desire expressed by Mr. Teissier?

MARIE

Yes, sir.

BOURDON

Of your own free will you have declined this proposal of marriage?

MARIE

Of my own free will.

BOURDON

Good! Good! I'm glad it's that way. For a moment, I was afraid, when you refused such a handsome offer, that your mother and sisters had conspired to keep you with them — not out of jealousy, but in a spirit of misdirected affection. If you have come to a definite, unalterable decision, of your own accord, I don't see any use in going further into the matter. (*A silence*)

MRS. VIGNERON

Don't be afraid, dear; answer frankly just what you think. (*Another silence*)

BOURDON

In case you regret your first decision, young lady — and that's easy to explain — I am offering you a chance to change your mind. You had better take advantage of it.

MARIE

You must tell Mr. Teissier for me that I like him better for his persistence, but that I still wish some time to think it over.

BOURDON

Well! That's a reasonable answer, madam — very sensible, indeed — That does n't look like the categorical refusal you gave me.

MRS. VIGNERON

My daughter may have changed her mind. But she should know that I don't approve of it.

BOURDON

Say no more, madam. Leave the young lady to her own devices. Later on she might reproach you because she followed your wishes. (*Returning to*

Marie) I understand perfectly, young lady, why
this marriage must present some objectionable fea-
tures to you, and why you have been in no hurry
to enter it.   Unfortunately, Teissier is not twenty
years old, like yourself — indeed, that is your greatest cause for complaint — and at his age, a man
is n't willing to have things delayed.

MARIE

Mr. Bourdon, I want to know, and I beg you will
tell me sincerely, whether Mr. Teissier is an honest
man.

BOURDON

An honest man! What do you mean by that? In
case you should marry Mr. Teissier, I should not
advise you to place implicit confidence in a simple
promise; but there are lawyers to draw up con-
tracts establishing the rights of the parties concerned. Have I answered your question?

MARIE

No; you did n't understand me. When a young
woman says " an honest man," she thinks of a good
many things.

BOURDON

Do you want to know whether Teissier has made his
money in an honorable way?

MARIE

Yes; I want to be assured on that point, as well as
some others.

BOURDON

Why should that worry you? If you were to look
into all the fortunes in France, there are n't a hundred — no, not fifty — that would stand a close examination. I speak as a man who has been through

the mill. Teissier has been in business all his life;
he has amassed a considerable sum, and nobody would
dream of attacking his right to it. That's all you
need to know.

MARIE

What is Mr. Teissier's ordinary conduct? What are
his tastes and his habits?

BOURDON

Just the tastes and habits of any man of his age. I
don't think you have anything to fear on that score.
I see now what you are driving at. Believe me, as a
husband Teissier will have rather too much than too
little virtue. I leave it to your mother.

MRS. VIGNERON

It occurs to me to ask what interest you have in this
marriage, Mr. Bourdon?

BOURDON

What interest, madam? Only the welfare of this
young lady, and yours, at the same time.

MRS. VIGNERON

It's rather late, is n't it, to show such devotion
for us?

BOURDON

Madam, you are still thinking of that wretched business. I know everything went about as badly as it
could. But was it my fault that you were unable
to fight for your husband's estate? You had to give
way to the law of the strongest, that's all. To-day,
this law has shifted in your favor. It happens that
your daughter has made a conquest of an old man,
who will grant anything to be able to spend his remaining days with her. The whole situation favors
you. You've got the trumps. Play 'em. Do I

need to tell you, madam, that we lawyers know neither the weak nor the strong; that absolute impartiality is a duty we never depart from? Nevertheless, I don't think I do wrong, even though I am Teissier's attorney, to stipulate for your daughter all the advantages she is in a position to demand. (*Returning to Marie*) You heard what I have just said to your mother, miss. Put whatever questions you wish to me; but particularly the question which is really the most important — the question of money. I'm listening.

MARIE

No; you speak.

BOURDON (*with a half-smile*)

I'm here to listen to you, and advise you.

MARIE

It would be painful for me to talk about it.

BOURDON (*smiling*)

Nonsense! What you want to know is what Mr. Teissier is worth, down to a cent, is n't it?

MARIE

It's enough, I know, without being told.

BOURDON

Right you are. Teissier is rich, very rich. Why, he's richer, the old fox, than he himself knows. Come, now, miss, I'm waiting for you.

MARIE

Of course Mr. Teissier has told you of his intentions?

BOURDON

Yes; but I must know yours, too. It's always fun for us lawyers to see the parties fighting tooth and nail over the terms.

MARIE

Please don't add to my embarrassment. If this marriage must take place, I had rather run my chances than make the conditions.

BOURDON (*smiling continually*)

Really! (*Marie looks at him fixedly*) I don't doubt your scruples, miss. When they are so plainly shown, we are forced to believe them sincere. But Teissier does n't think you are marrying him for his beauty. So he is already willing to make a settlement on you. But this settlement, I hasten to tell you, is not sufficient. You are making a bargain, are you not? Or, if that word hurts you, at any rate a speculation. And you ought to reap all the benefits of it. So it is only just — and you can insist — that when Teissier marries you, he shall make you half-owner of all he possesses, irrevocably and incontestably, so that you will receive one-half after he dies. Then all you would have to do would be to pray that time would not be too long deferred. (*Turning to Mrs. Vigneron*) You heard what I have just told your daughter, madam?

MRS. VIGNERON

I heard.

BOURDON

What do you think?

MRS. VIGNERON

If you want to know, Mr. Bourdon, I think instead of promising my daughter half Mr. Teissier's fortune, you would have done better to have saved for her that of her father's.

BOURDON

Can't get away from that subject, eh, madam? (*Returning to Marie*) Well, miss, now you know the great advantages in store for you in the near future. I am wondering what objections you can find now. I can't think of any. Sentimental objections? I am speaking, I think, to a sensible young woman, well brought up, without foolish notions. You ought to know there is no such thing as love. I never met with it. This world is made up of businesses. Marriage is a business, just like the rest, and the chances offered you to-day will never come your way again.

MARIE

In the conversations you have had with Mr. Teissier, has he said anything about my family?

BOURDON

About your family? No. (*In a low tone*) Do they want something, too?

MARIE

Mr. Teissier ought to know that I would never consent to separate from them.

BOURDON

Why should you? Your sisters are nice girls, and your mother is very agreeable. Besides, Teissier has every reason not to want to leave a young wife with idle moments on her hands. Now, miss, be ready for what remains for me to tell you. Teissier came here with me. He is outside. He is waiting for a reply, and this time it must be a definite answer. You will take long chances in doing otherwise. So it is a "yes" or "no" that I am asking for.

MRS. VIGNERON

That's enough of that, Mr. Bourdon. I was willing
enough for you to tell my daughter whatever propo-
sitions were made to her. Whether she accepts them
or not, is her business. But I don't intend that she
shall be surprised into acceptance, or do anything
in a moment of weakness or emotion. Moreover, you
must know that I reserve the right to have a talk with
her and tell her certain things which would be out of
place with you here — things a mother can tell her
child, and must tell, when they are alone. One thing
I can tell you: I have n't brought up a girl to be
twenty — a girl full of health and fine spirit — only
to hand her over to an old man.

BOURDON

To whom are you going to give her? To hear you
talk, madam, anyone might think you had your
pockets full of sons-in-law, and that your daughters'
only trouble was to choose between them. Why was
it that the marriage of one of them — a marriage
that seemed practically settled — fell through? Lack
of money. And lack of money, madam, is just what
will keep every one of your daughters an old maid.

MRS. VIGNERON

You're wrong. I had nothing, and neither did my
husband. He married me all the same, and we have
been very happy.

BOURDON

It is true you have had four children. But if your
husband were still in this world, madam, he would
disagree with you — perhaps for the first time.
When he saw the situation of his daughters, he would
be frightened — for, whatever you may think of it,

it is perplexing and dangerous. He would put a true value on Mr. Teissier's proposal. To be sure, it is not perfect; but it is more than acceptable. It is reassuring for the present and (*looking at Marie*) full of dazzling prospects for the future. I know well enough that it's easy to say what dead people might or might n't do, but this young lady's father, whose heart was just as big as yours, had all the experience that you lack. He knew life. He knew that you pay for what you get in this world. And, in the end, his thoughts to-day would be something like this: "I have lived for my family; I died for them; surely my daughter can sacrifice a few years for them."

MARIE (*with her eyes full of tears*)

Tell Mr. Teissier I accept.

BOURDON

Come now, young lady, you're giving yourself a good deal of trouble over making your fortune. Here is your contract. I drew it up in advance, without knowing whether I should be paid for my trouble. Read it over carefully and soberly. All it needs is Teissier's signature; and I 'll attend to that. I was your father's lawyer, and I 'm hoping to be yours. I 'll go find Teissier and bring him here. (*He goes out*)

MARIE (*to her mother*)

Kiss me — but don't say anything. Don't take away my courage. I 've no more than I need, as it is. You must see that Mr. Bourdon is right. This marriage is our salvation. I 'm ashamed — oh, so ashamed! — to do it; but I should always feel guilty if I did not. Mother dear, could you, at your age

begin to live another life of misery and privation?
Yes, yes, I know — you are full of courage! But
Blanche — Blanche, the poor child — we can't ask
her to have courage — not her.   What remorse I
should have to suffer later, if her health were to
demand care that we could n't give her! And Judith!
Oh, I 'm thinking of Judith, too. Who knows what
would become of a young girl, the best, the highest-
minded girl in the world, if she should be driven to
extremes, and should lose her fear — of things.
Come, I feel a weight off my shoulders now that it 's
done.   It will be just as he wishes — a dishonest,
self-seeking marriage — and a sad one, too.   But
still I prefer a little shame and regret that I know
about to a host of terrors of all kinds that might
end in a terrible misfortune. Don't cry any more;
don't let them see that you have been crying.

[*Bourdon comes in, followed by Teissier. Teissier,
smiling, goes toward Marie; but Bourdon stops him
and motions that he must first speak to Mrs.
Vigneron.*

TEISSIER

How do you do, madam. (*Going to Marie*) Is it
really true, what Bourdon just told me — that you
will be my wife?

MARIE

It is true.

TEISSIER

A mighty good decision — you won't change your
mind by to-morrow, will you? (*She offers him her
hand; he kisses her on both cheeks*) Don't blush.
That 's the way we do in the village I came from.
A man kisses his bride-to-be first on the right cheek,

saying, " Here 's one for the Mayor "; and then one
on the left cheek, saying, " Here 's one for the
priest." (*Marie smiles; Teissier goes over to Mrs.
Vigneron*) If you are willing, madam, we 'll publish
the banns to-morrow. Bourdon will make us a little
contract — won't you, Bourdon? (*Bourdon replies
with a significant gesture*) And three weeks from now
your second daughter will be Mrs. Teissier.

[*Rosalie enters.*

MRS. VIGNERON

What is it, Rosalie?

ROSALIE

Will you see Mr. Dupuis, ma'am?

MRS. VIGNERON

Mr. Dupuis? The house-furnisher?

ROSALIE

Yes, ma'am.

MRS. VIGNERON

What does he want of us?

ROSALIE

You owe him money, ma'am. At least, he says so.
Another vulture, sure as you live!

MRS. VIGNERON

We owe Mr. Dupuis nothing — do you hear? —
nothing! Tell him I don't want to see him.

TEISSIER

Yes, madam, yes; you must see Mr. Dupuis. Either
there is really something due him, in spite of what
you think, or Mr. Dupuis is mistaken, in which case
it won't be out of place to show him his error. You
are not alone; you have a man with you now. Show
Mr. Dupuis in. Miss Marie is going to receive him.

She will soon be mistress of a house, and I want to see how she will act. Come, Bourdon. Let's leave your daughter with Mr. Dupuis.

[*Mrs. Vigneron and Bourdon go out at the left.*

TEISSIER (*to Marie*)

I'll be here, behind this door; I won't miss a word. (*He hides behind the door*)

DUPUIS (*entering*)

How do you do, Miss Marie.

MARIE

How do you do, Mr. Dupuis.

DUPUIS

Is your mother well?

MARIE

Pretty well, thank you.

DUPUIS

Your sisters are well?

MARIE

Yes.

DUPUIS

I don't need to ask how you are; you're as fresh and rosy as a new-born babe.

MARIE

My mother told me to receive you for her, Mr. Dupuis. Tell me as soon as possible what brings you here.

DUPUIS

Can't you make a little guess as to what brings me here?

MARIE

No, really.

DUPUIS

Is that so? Don't you say to yourself, that if I
come here, after so long a time has passed, it must
be that I need money?

MARIE

Explain yourself.

DUPUIS

I would have given a whole lot — yes, I would, young
lady — not to have to make this visit. When I
heard of your father's death, I said to my wife:
" I believe Mr. Vigneron still owes us something —
but what of it? — it is n't much, and we won't die
if we set it down to profit and loss." That 's the way
I do with my good customers. Mr. Vigneron was a
good customer; never had the least trouble with
him; that 's the way things ought to be between
honest folks. Unfortunately, you know how business
is — up one day and down the next; well, it is n't
good just now. Understand?

MARIE

I 'm pretty certain, Mr. Dupuis, that my father
settled everything with you.

DUPUIS

Don't say that — you hurt me.

MARIE

Nevertheless, I 'm as sure as anyone can be that my
father squared his account with you.

DUPUIS

Be careful; you 'll get me angry. It 's only a matter of two thousand francs. The amount is n't worth
the trouble. Perhaps you are embarrassed at this
moment. Then say so. I have n't come to take your
last cent. Just let your mother give me a note for

two thousand francs, at three months. Her signature is the same as ready money to me.

MARIE

I 'll tell my mother you are here to collect two thousand francs. But I tell you again you are mistaken. I 'm certain we don't owe it.

DUPUIS

Well, young lady, I don't leave here till I get it. I came politely, with my hat in my hand (*he puts it on*) and you seem to be treating me like a robber. Those ways don't go with me. You 'd better find your mother and make her give me two thousand francs — or a note — I 'm still willing to take her note — or Mr. Dupuis will have a fit of anger that will shake the house.

[*Teissier enters; Dupuis, surprised and quickly intimidated by his appearance, takes off his hat again.*

TEISSIER

Keep your hat on. There 's no ceremony in business. You 've got your bill with you?

DUPUIS

Certainly, sir, I have my bill.

TEISSIER

Let 's have it.

DUPUIS

Shall I give my bill to this gentleman, miss?

MARIE

Do as he says.

TEISSIER (*reading the bill*)

" Received of Mrs. Vigneron, two thousand francs to settle her account in full." What kind of a bill is this? Don't you usually give an itemized account?

DUPUIS

We can't make out the same bill five or six times,
sir. The first one I rendered to Mr. Vigneron contained all the necessary specifications.

TEISSIER

All right. I'm going to pay you. I'll verify the
bill when I get home.

DUPUIS

Go ahead, sir, and verify it. Mr. Vigneron should
have left his papers in order.

TEISSIER

Yes, he did. (*Holding the bill close to his eyes*)
Dupuis is the name, eh? Is this signature yours?
You are Mr. Dupuis?

DUPUIS

Yes, sir.

TEISSIER

I am going to give you your two thousand francs.

DUPUIS

Verify it, sir, if you can. I'll wait till then.

TEISSIER

You're very sure that when Mr. Vigneron died, he
still owed you two thousand francs?

DUPUIS

Yes, sir — yes, sir. My wife may have made a mistake in her figures; but I don't think so.

TEISSIER

Your wife has nothing to do with it. It's you who
would be liable if you received the same amount twice.

DUPUIS

I don't demand it, sir, if it isn't due me. I am an
honest man.

TEISSIER (*offering him the money*)

Here's your two thousand francs.

DUPUIS

No; verify it first. I'd rather you would.

TEISSIER

Get out of here! And don't let me see you inside
these doors again. Do you hear?

DUPUIS

What's that, sir?

TEISSIER

I tell you not to come back here. Don't be fresh,
or you'll regret it.

DUPUIS

Give me back my bill, anyway.

TEISSIER

Look out, or you'll see it again in a courtroom.

DUPUIS

Now that's too much! How dare you — I don't
even know who you are — how dare you talk to me
like that! I'm going, miss; but you'll hear from
me again — and soon! (*He puts on his hat and
goes out*)

TEISSIER

Child, since your father died you've been surrounded
by a lot of scoundrels. . . . Let's go and join your
family.

CURTAIN

THE WOMAN OF PARIS

(LA PARISIENNE)

A COMEDY IN THREE ACTS

1885

PERSONS

Clotilde
Adèle
Du Mesnil
Lafont
Simpson

The play takes place in Paris.

THE WOMAN OF PARIS

THE FIRST ACT

An elegantly furnished drawing-room. At the rear, two double doors. At the right, a window. There are side doors: a double one, halfway back, at the right; a single one at the left, in the foreground. At the right, against the wall, a writing-desk. On the left side, near the front of the stage, is a centre-table, with a blotting-pad upon it. Other furniture, mirrors, flowers, etc.

When the curtain rises, there is nobody on the stage. Clotilde, dressed for the street, gloved and with her hat on, comes in hurriedly at the rear door. She has a letter in her hand; she goes to the centre-table, raises the blotter and hides the letter under it. Then she goes to the writing-desk, at the same time taking a bunch of keys from her pocket. At this moment Lafont appears. He sees her at the desk. She pretends to be closing the desk quickly. Lafont puts down his hat with evident emotion and goes over to Clotilde. He restrains his feelings with difficulty.

LAFONT

Open the desk and give me that letter!

CLOTILDE

No.   [*Pause.*

LAFONT

Open the desk and give me that letter!

CLOTILDE

I don't want to.

[*Another, and longer pause.*

LAFONT

Where have you been?

CLOTILDE

Oh, so now it's something else?

LAFONT

Yes, it's something else. I want to know where you have been.

CLOTILDE

I'm going to tell you. But first I want you to look in the glass and see the face you are making at me. You don't look beautiful. I like you better as you usually are. Good heavens! what's going to happen if you lose your head entirely over a miserable note sent by the first person that happens along?

LAFONT

Open that desk and give me the letter.

CLOTILDE

You're going to see it. . . . You ought to know that if we are to have many scenes like this, I'll be through with you pretty quickly. I warn you I'm not going to submit to an examination every time I set foot outdoors.

LAFONT

Where have you been?

CLOTILDE

Now try at least to show some sense, please! It isn't likely that if I had just left somebody, I'd find a letter from him as soon as I got in the house.

LAFONT

Open that desk and give me the letter.

CLOTILDE

Perhaps you are joking?

LAFONT

I don't look like it, do I?

CLOTILDE

You're suspicious of me, then?

LAFONT

That's more like it. (*He points at the desk*)

CLOTILDE

You want me to? You insist? You demand it? All right. (*She fumbles slowly, for the sake of appearances, in the pocket of her dress; first she takes out a handkerchief; then she throws the keys at him*) Open it yourself. (*He walks away and stands still, undecided, fretful*) Come, pull yourself together and open it. When you begin a thing, you'd better see it through. Show you're a man. (*He makes up his mind, goes toward the keys and stoops to pick them up; she approaches him*) Be careful what you do. If you just touch those keys — just with the tips of your fingers — you'll be sorry for it, not I.

LAFONT (*after some hesitation, picks up the keys and hands them to her*) Take your keys.

[*There is a moment's pause while Clotilde takes off her hat and gloves, and makes herself comfortable.*

CLOTILDE

That makes it all the worse, you know.

LAFONT

Makes what worse?

CLOTILDE

The trouble is growing. I warn you.

LAFONT

What trouble?

CLOTILDE

I knew you were watching me, and I laughed at the trouble you took — all for nothing. Up to now I have n't said anything about it. It was jealousy; but a kind of jealousy that flatters a woman's vanity and amuses her. Now you 've gone over to the other kind of jealousy — stupid, tawdry, brutal jealousy, that makes a woman feel bad. We don't forgive that kind the second time.

LAFONT

Clotilde!

CLOTILDE

Going to begin again?

LAFONT

No.

CLOTILDE

Good for you!

LAFONT

Clotilde!

CLOTILDE

What is it, my friend?

LAFONT

You love me?

CLOTILDE

Not so much as I did yesterday.

LAFONT

You want me to be happy?

CLOTILDE

I think I 've shown you whether I do or not.

LAFONT

I 'm afraid of all those young fellows that swarm around you.

CLOTILDE

You 're utterly mistaken. I talk with all of them,
but no sooner are their backs turned than I can't
remember one from the other.

LAFONT

Can't you remember a single one whom you might
have encouraged thoughtlessly, and who might think
he could write to you?

CLOTILDE

Not one.

LAFONT (*begging*)

Open the desk and give me that letter.

CLOTILDE

Still at it! That letter is from a friend of mine,
Mrs. Doyen-Beaulieu — (*Lafont starts*) the most
proper woman alive — in spite of her free and easy
ways. I remember what Pauline wrote, and I should
have told you about it, if you had n't asked me.

LAFONT

Clotilde!

CLOTILDE

Go on.

LAFONT

Are you reasonable?

CLOTILDE

More than ever.

LAFONT

Is your mind calm?

CLOTILDE

My mind is calm; and so is my heart.

LAFONT

Think of me, Clotilde, and think of yourself. Remember, it 's easy to do foolish things, but they can

never be undone. Don't give way to this mania for adventures, which craves so many victims nowadays. Resist it, Clotilde, resist it. As long as you are faithful to me, you are good and honorable; the day you deceive me . . .

CLOTILDE (*stops him, goes a little way toward the second rear door and then comes back*) Look out; here's my husband!

DU MESNIL (*entering*)

I knew it was Lafont I heard! How you do go on, chattering and gossiping, when you are together. Thunder would n't stop you.

CLOTILDE (*going to him, and speaking in a low voice*) So you 're back?

DU MESNIL

Yes; I 'm back again.

CLOTILDE

Have you been here long?

DU MESNIL

Some little time.

CLOTILDE

It seems to me when one of your friends is here, you could show yourself and entertain him.

DU MESNIL

I was finishing something.

CLOTILDE

What did your uncle have to say to you?

DU MESNIL

I did n't see him.

CLOTILDE

He 's hard to get at.

DU MESNIL

He sent word for me to come again to-day.

CLOTILDE

Want me to go with you?

DU MESNIL

You 'd only be in the way.

CLOTILDE

Thanks.

DU MESNIL (*going to Lafont and offering his hand*)

How are you?

LAFONT

Pretty well. And you?

DU MESNIL

Hang it, I 'm not in particularly good spirits just now.

LAFONT

What 's the trouble?

DU MESNIL

I work too hard, and it affects my health.

LAFONT

Take a rest then.

DU MESNIL

A fellow has to have time and money to take a rest.

LAFONT

You earn the money.

DU MESNIL

I get it one minute and spend it the next.

LAFONT

That must be fun.

DU MESNIL

It is — when you 're young.

CLOTILDE

Now stop your whining, will you! Do you suppose Mr. Lafont is interested? Do you think I like it? What 's the use of all this complaining? Your appe-

tite is all right. You sleep well enough. And I don't
know of a husband that's pampered as you are.
You work! Of course you work! Everybody works!
If I were you, I'd do four times as much work and
not talk about it one-fortieth as much.

DU MESNIL

She's a corker, my wife is. You don't know, old
chap, what it is to have a house like mine, where the
bills grow bigger every year, and we acquire costlier
habits every day.

CLOTILDE

Any more?

DU MESNIL

Let me talk a little. I didn't interrupt you, just
now. If you're such a busy bee, sit down and do
some work. Have a look at your children's knicker-
bockers; the poor things are always out at the seat
of their breeches.

CLOTILDE

I spoil them.

DU MESNIL

But you don't mend them enough.

CLOTILDE

That's the chambermaid's job.

DU MESNIL

We're living as simply as we can. It costs me a neat
little sum, I tell you, and the place is a regular
prison! Nowadays servants aren't satisfied with
wages; they have to have salaries. True enough,
we dine in town frequently — almost every day. But
my wife, of course, wants to be dressed like the rest,
so what we save on one thing is spent on another.

There's one thing, though; we get better things to eat.

CLOTILDE

There's where you are right.

DU MESNIL

I don't deny it.   I'd rather have a good meal outside than a poor one at home.

CLOTILDE (*going toward him*)

Now stop it, please, and let's talk about something more agreeable.

DU MESNIL

You're a bachelor, Lafont.   Well, take my advice and stay so.

LAFONT

Is that what you think, Mrs. Du Mesnil?

CLOTILDE

Get married or not;   that's your business.   (*She walks away*)

DU MESNIL

I hope you'll be more agreeable than my wife, and listen to what I want to tell you?

LAFONT

Fire away.

DU MESNIL

Right at this very moment there are big things on foot for me;   things mighty well worth while.

LAFONT

Tell me about them.

DU MESNIL

It's my uncle, my uncle Jean-Baptiste, the member of the Academy, who's at the bottom of it.   For a long time he hasn't been satisfied with my situation.

He wants me to go back into the Treasury Department. He has friends there, and most of them know
me; and these gentlemen are trying to work me into
a certain collectorship.

LAFONT

That 's the kind of a job for you, where you 'd
have plenty of time and be under obligations to
nobody.

DU MESNIL

I 'm not doing so badly now. I 'm in high favor with
the agricultural societies. They never issue a statement without submitting it to me first. My contri-
butions to the Agricultural Bulletin — I spring a
sensation there now and then — are pretty well received. They 're making me known. I take whatever comes along. But my uncle does n't see it that
way. He thinks that at my age, with a wife and
children, a man ought to have a fixed position.

LAFONT

He 's right.

DU MESNIL

Perhaps he is. I 'm not a mathematician, nor an
economist; I 'm — well, I 'm not those. Between
you and me, my little book, " The Moral Aspects of
the Appropriation Bill," made something of a hit.
The book appeals only to the most intellectual
readers, and of course it does n't go like a best-seller.
But up to now one hundred and nineteen copies of
" Moral Aspects " have been sold — or one hundred
and eighteen. There 's one copy we can't find. Perhaps somebody stole it. I seem to see in all this a
new sphere of effort for me — a new vein to work.

LAFONT

You 'd better see about the collectorship first. That 's the surest thing; after that you can do what you please. I 'll see what I can do myself, to give you a boost.

DU MESNIL

Be very careful. My uncle has got this business well in hand, and he wants to settle it alone, with his friends. It strikes me that when a member of the Academy of Moral and Political Sciences is willing to ask a favor; when he is asking it for his nephew; when that nephew is somebody — the government can't do anything but grant it. Does n't it strike you that way?

LAFONT

There are n't always places to be had.

DU MESNIL

I know there will be soon.

LAFONT

Tell me — it 's sure they 've promised you a collectorship in Paris?

DU MESNIL

In Paris, of course. My wife could n't live in the country.

[*During this conversation Clotilde has sat down near the table. She has taken the letter from beneath the blotter and, taking advantage of the fact that her husband's back is turned to her, she has shown it several times to Lafont with a gesture signifying: " Look at this! " This business should be so timed that the last words of Du Mesnil, " My wife could n't live in the country," come right on top of it.*]

CLOTILDE (*having risen*)

Adolphe, read this letter.

DU MESNIL (*turning round*)

What does it say?

CLOTILDE

Open it and see.   (*Handing him the letter*)   It 's
from Pauline.

DU MESNIL (*reading*)

" My dear — you are going to receive, if you have n't
already, an invitation to Mrs. Simpson's grand ball,
on the 25th.   Your self-respect has been in good
hands, and has not been made to suffer.   I uttered
your name, she caught it, saying she knew you well,
that you were a very nice person, and that she would
be charmed to have you at her parties.   So you 're
on the inside now — I 'm quite sure you will like my
friend, and that you will get along well together.
It 's a fact, she is n't so young as she used to be.
You tell me what age you *think* she is, and I will tell
you how old she really *is*.   But just the same, when
she is dressed for the ball, décolletée, with all her
diamonds on, Mrs. Simpson, though no longer queen
of the ball, can still make a hit.   Such arms!   And
eyes!   A way of smiling I never saw the like of!
And so easy-going!   Nothing shocks her.   She understands every weakness.   There 's no frivolity,
no matter how far it may go, that does n't seem
interesting or excusable to her."

[*Du Mesnil, uneasy and shocked, turns to Lafont.
The latter, still more affected, returns the look; they
exchange expressions of vexation, nodding their
heads in unison several times.*

DU MESNIL (*going over the letter*)

"And so easy-going!" (*He looks at Lafont, and they go through the same business*) "Nothing shocks her!" (*Same business*) "She understands every weakness!" (*Same business*) "There's no frivolity, however far it may go" . . . (*Going over to Clotilde, who thus is placed between the two men; Du Mesnil on her right*) I don't think much of that letter of Pauline's.

LAFONT (*at the left*)

Your friend is rather inconsistent, Mrs. Du Mesnil.

DU MESNIL

There you see! I know this Mrs. Simpson. They tell some queer stories about her.

LAFONT

Mrs. Simpson has a deplorable reputation.

DU MESNIL

You hear, don't you? I don't want you to visit a house that might compromise you.

LAFONT

I assure you, it is no place for you, among a lot of women of doubtful reputation.

DU MESNIL

Well? It ought to mean something to you to see Lafont and me of exactly the same mind.

CLOTILDE

All right. We'll do whatever you please. (*With a look at Lafont*) If we aren't going to Mrs. Simpson's, we'll go somewhere else, that's all. But in the future, please wait till we are alone, before speaking of certain things. I'm not accustomed to take advice from strangers. (*She moves away from them abruptly*)

DU MESNIL

What's that? Lafont! A stranger? (*To Lafont*)
So you've had a row with Clotilde?

LAFONT

No, it's you. Since you've been here, you've stirred
her up unnecessarily.

DU MESNIL (*going over to Clotilde*)

I'm going.

CLOTILDE (*dryly*)

Good luck!

DU MESNIL

What are you going to do to-day?

CLOTILDE

Whatever I please.

DU MESNIL

Where'll we dine this evening?

CLOTILDE

I know nothing about that.

DU MESNIL

What kind of a way is that to answer me?

CLOTILDE

I'm going to be careful what I say to a quarrel-
some, disobliging man.

DU MESNIL

So you think it's a good thing to go to this ball?

CLOTILDE

I don't care a snap about this ball. I had already
forgotten it. I'm no débutante, I guess, to go wild
about any particular ball. But you've got to complain! You've got to whine! You haul your wife
over the coals without the slightest regard for her
feelings! Anyone that heard you would get a pretty

poor idea — and a false idea, too — of our home life.

DU MESNIL

I was only fooling, girlie! Don't be mad at me. There are a lot of husbands like me. I growl around for about three seconds, and when you 've made up your mind what you want, that 's what finally happens. Who 's the boss here? (*She smiles*) My mind is full of this collectorship. It would be a great thing for us. We ought to think more about it. Come, Clotilde, looking at it in the light of reason, do you think I 'll get it?

CLOTILDE

We 'll see.

DU MESNIL

I 've got my degrees, have n't I?

CLOTILDE

Degrees? They 're no good.

DU MESNIL

I 've got the support of able men.

CLOTILDE

Without any influence.

DU MESNIL

Don't you think the good-will of the Academy is a strong point?

CLOTILDE

You may be wrong in not wanting me to meddle with the business.

DU MESNIL

What would you do?

CLOTILDE

A thousand things that are no trouble to a woman, and give her a chance to go around a little. I should put all my women friends to work; Pauline first of all. Pauline likes you very much. She even wishes her husband were like you! Pauline, who is hand in glove with Mrs. Simpson, would get her interested in our affairs. When you don't want to go to Mrs. Simpson's, you make me laugh. What does she care for us? She receives the best people in Paris. She always has two or three diplomats at her table. She would have you to dinner with them. You would tell them what you have in mind — you could speak confidently, as man to man, smoking those big cigars you are so fond of. Then, when otherwise the " powers that be " would be telling you: " We 're sorry, but the place has already been disposed of " — then you would be able to say: " I know it has — the appointment is in my pocket now." That 's the way I look at this business.

DU MESNIL

Perhaps you 're right. But wait. Don't let us be rash. If at any time I see that things are going badly, and that my resources are insufficient, then we can always try your way.

CLOTILDE

Whenever you like. . . . (*Whispers*) You know the way I get around *you*. (*They laugh*)

DU MESNIL

I 'm going to see my uncle. Shall I take Lafont with me, or will you keep him here?

CLOTILDE

I 'll keep him here. He provokes me, but he amuses me, too. I always have to laugh at his nose. (*They laugh*)

DU MESNIL

You treat poor Lafont badly.   And he is so friendly and obliging.

CLOTILDE (*in her husband's ear*)

I should n't care to be kissed by a man with a nose like his. (*They laugh*)

DU MESNIL (*going over to Lafont*)

Well, so long! You 'd better not come with me, if I 'm as disagreeable as my wife says I am.   You don't know what it is to have a wife and children. A fellow loves them a whole lot, and is always thinking about them, and finds time hanging heavy when they 're not around; but all that does n't prevent him at times from wishing them to the devil. (*He goes out*)

CLOTILDE

There you can see that we have to be a little careful. If my husband had come in a minute earlier, it would have been all up with me. (*A pause*)

LAFONT

You are making a fool of me.

CLOTILDE

Why so?

LAFONT

With that letter. (*She laughs*) It would have been so easy to show it to me at once.

CLOTILDE

I thought you would n't like it, and I was right. Besides, it was a trap I set for you.   I wanted to see if you 'd stop in time.

LAFONT

To fall into it another time.

CLOTILDE

That's it exactly. You are very foolish, my friend, and your surmises are not very fortunate either. Come now, I want to do something for you, though you don't deserve it a bit. My husband opens all my letters; all of them, every last one. Don't worry about that; I prefer it so. Sit down and let's talk awhile, please. We can talk without quarrelling, can't we? What with my husband on one side, and with you on the other, I get rather too much of it in a single day. Won't you tell me what is rankling in you; what the meaning is of this jealousy that has become so alarming? It got hold of you all of a sudden, without warning . . . about the 15th of January. (*He looks at her; she smiles*) I have reason for remembering that date.

LAFONT

What reason?

CLOTILDE

I have one, that's enough. Now we're not going to discuss every word. Come — you talk — I'm listening.

LAFONT (*after hesitating*)

Where have you been?

CLOTILDE (*laughing*)

That's right — I owe you an apology, my friend. I forgot you had asked me that question several times, and that I hadn't answered it. I had an appointment — don't lose your head about it! — with my milliner. You don't meet very many men there, I assure you. Surely you will let me go to my milliner's now and then. Now do what I tell you, and answer my question. Let me know how I have wronged you. I always find it so hard to discover it myself.

LAFONT

I don't see much of you these days.

CLOTILDE

Nonsense! What are you doing now? Am I not here? If you want to waste on discussions and quarrelling the time we could put in more agreeably — that's your loss.

LAFONT

I waited for you all this week . . . last week, too . . . and the week before that, too. . . .

CLOTILDE

Fiddledeedee! Why not a year? When you had waited that long, and I had broken my word with you, not once, but a hundred times, then you'd have good cause to imagine terrible things. Can I always do as I please? Am I not dependent on everybody in this house? (*Touching his arm*) You don't seem to realize that I'm married. . . . No; there's something else. I want you to tell me what it is.

LAFONT

It seems to me that you are getting tired of our friendship . . . that you are looking for something new, and perhaps you have found it . . . that we are at the inevitable moment when lying begins . . . and bad faith . . . and the rest of the nasty little tricks.

CLOTILDE

I don't know when all those nice things begin. You are better informed than I on that point. I'm asking you for facts — straight, brief, definite — something I might meet with a single word. Do you

want an answer to what goes on in your imagination?
Your imagination does n't seem to me very joyous or
full of pleasant memories.

LAFONT

That date . . . the 15th of January . . . which
you are so exact about. . . .

CLOTILDE (*more attentive*)

Well, that date?

LAFONT

I seem to remember it, too.

CLOTILDE

Own up now, that you don't remember anything of
the kind. I should n't have put the date in your head.
It means something to me, but nothing at all to you.

LAFONT

I 've noticed other things besides.

CLOTILDE

What are they?

LAFONT

Oh, a lot of things.

CLOTILDE

What things?

LAFONT

Oh, nothing; they 're — well, intuitions. But you
can't fool with intuitions.

CLOTILDE

Well, trot out some of your intuitions, and let 's
look at them.

LAFONT

You 've changed a good deal, my dear, without giving
any explanation. For one thing, you make fun of
me. That is n't polite. I find you absent-minded
very often; and very often embarrassed, too. I see

that you 're hiding from me what you have been doing; and I 'm afraid to ask you. Sometimes you
contradict yourself. . . .

CLOTILDE

How surprising!

LAFONT

You talk to me about people who live in another
world than yours, and you know their comings and
goings by heart. How? It 's you now that tell me
the current scandal — I used to have the fun of telling you. And your political opinions are not the
same!

CLOTILDE

What a child you are! And so am I, too, for taking
you seriously. My political opinions! You mean
that I am a reactionary? I have n't changed. Oh,
yes, in that way; yes, you 're right — I am a good
reactionary. I like peace and order and old, estab-
lished principles. I want the churches to remain
open, in case I should take it into my head to go
to them. I want the stores to be open, too, and full
of pretty things. I like to look at them even if I
can't buy them. But even supposing my political
opinions should have become modified, it seems to me
that you are the last one who has a right to complain
of that. You don't despise the new things that are
coming up. You are a democrat. But, of course,
that 's a fad which does n't commit you to anything
these days. One finds democrats in all parties.
You 're a freethinker! Why, I believe you could get
along with a mistress who had no religion at all.
It 's disgusting! . . . What was it my husband had
to tell you, if I may ask?

LAFONT

He spoke of a position he wants to get, and perhaps will get.

CLOTILDE

Were you interested?

LAFONT

Very much.

CLOTILDE

You say " very much " just as you would say " not the least." How do you think my husband looks?

LAFONT

Very well.

CLOTILDE

He does n't strike you as care-worn or tired?

LAFONT

No.

CLOTILDE

Never mind. I don't know why I speak of Adolph to you, seeing how you feel toward him. But it does n't matter. Here is what I was getting at. You know my husband is looking for a position; it goes without saying he 's looking to the government for it. Whatever the government may be, when you 're looking for a place, you have to make your application to it. And you think I am going to criticize the government just when our affairs are at stake? That 's what a man would do. A man chatters so much; a man is so clumsy and ungrateful! Women are never like that. . . . Do you want me to tell you what 's the matter with you? You 've given way to a miserable feeling of self-interest. Probably you thought, in going ahead the way you have, that you 'd find out something; but you don't know any-

thing, and you won't know anything — because
there's nothing to know. It's a lesson for me,
though. Meanwhile, bear this in mind: you must be
prudent, and patient, and have confidence, and be satisfied with what I can give you, without demanding
the impossible. You ought to realize that I'm not
free to do as I please. I have a house to look after,
and appearances to keep up. Pleasure comes in the
second place. Remember, too, that the least outburst
from you might compromise me, and if my husband
should ever learn anything, I don't know what he'd
do with me. Now understand me, once for all: I
don't want to find you again as you were to-day —
planted right in front of my door, waving your hands
and ready to eat everybody alive — when I get back
from a quiet little visit to my dressmaker. (*Lafont,
who has heard all this with bowed head, suddenly
looks up*) Well? What's the matter now?

LAFONT

Where have you been?

CLOTILDE

I just told you.

LAFONT

Is it your milliner or your dressmaker you've just
come from?

CLOTILDE

Why?

LAFONT

Answer me. Is it your milliner or dressmaker you've
just come from?

CLOTILDE

I've seen both of them. There, are you satisfied?
. . . Now you must be going.

LAFONT
No.

CLOTILDE
Yes.

LAFONT
In a little while.

CLOTILDE
Right now.

LAFONT
What 's your hurry?

CLOTILDE
I 'm in no hurry.

LAFONT
Let me stay then.

CLOTILDE
Impossible. If my husband comes back and finds you still here, he might be seriously angry. Come, be sensible and say good-bye. Next time you 'll do less talking.

LAFONT
Clotilde?

CLOTILDE
What is it now?

LAFONT
I 'm going back to my house.

CLOTILDE
Go ahead; I 'm not stopping you.

LAFONT
You know what time it is?

CLOTILDE
About.

LAFONT
The day is n't over yet.

CLOTILDE

It won't begin again.

LAFONT

All you have to do is put on your hat; that is n't
much.

CLOTILDE

I thought that 's what you were getting at. I 'd be
very much surprised if all your talk ended any other
way.

LAFONT

Put on your hat, will you?

CLOTILDE

Very well. That 's the only good idea you 've had
lately. I may as well take advantage of it. Go ahead.

LAFONT

You 'll come after me?

CLOTILDE

I 'll be with you.

LAFONT

Soon?

CLOTILDE

In a few minutes. But run along now.

LAFONT

Immediately?

CLOTILDE

Immediately. (*He goes out*)
[*Clotilde rings.*

ADÈLE (*entering*)

Did you ring, ma'am?

CLOTILDE

Adèle, give me my dressing-gown and slippers. I 'm
not going out again.

CURTAIN

THE SECOND ACT

The scene is the same as in the first act.

CLOTILDE (*dressed and ready to go out, is giving one last glance at herself in the glass*) Do I look all right, Adèle?

ADÈLE
Yes, ma'am.

CLOTILDE
Very well?

ADÈLE
Very well, ma'am.

CLOTILDE
What time is it?

ADÈLE
Almost three o'clock, ma'am.

CLOTILDE
Is everything I need on this table?

ADÈLE
All you usually take. Your keys, note-book, and box of rice powder.

CLOTILDE
Give them to me.

ADÈLE (*with a knowing air*)
You won't be back to-day, ma'am, will you?

CLOTILDE

Possibly not.

ADÈLE (*in the same tone*)

Probably not?

CLOTILDE

Why probably?

ADÈLE

Mr. Du Mesnil is dining at the Economist Club. He
would n't quit there for a king's ransom.

CLOTILDE

Well, what of it?

ADÈLE

I 've noticed that on such occasions you pass the
day with your — your schoolmate — the one Mr.
Du Mesnil has never seen.

CLOTILDE

So you 've been listening?

ADÈLE

No, ma'am, I don't listen. . . . I 've caught a few
words here and there, that 's all. . . . I 've already
told you, ma'am, that my brother . . .

CLOTILDE

Oh, yes, I know all about that brother! You want
to go out. All right, go on.

ADÈLE

Thank you, ma'am. (*Clotilde goes toward the rear
door*) There 's nothing else you want, ma'am?

CLOTILDE

No. Don't let the cook go out, and ask her to be
within reach when Mr. Du Mesnil comes home to
dress.

ADÈLE

Yes, ma'am. Shall I call a carriage, ma'am?

CLOTILDE

You need n't bother. I 'll get one on my way.

ADÈLE (*following Clotilde*)

Good-bye, ma'am. . . . Enjoy yourself.

[*When they reach the door they are halted abruptly by the sound of the door-bell. A pause.*

ADÈLE

Somebody 's ringing, ma'am.

CLOTILDE

I know it. (*Retracing her steps*) Three o'clock! He has n't seen me for a long time! He knows the Economist Club dinner is to-day. I ought to have expected he would have a relapse.

[*There is a second ring at the bell.*

ADÈLE

What shall I do, ma'am?

CLOTILDE

Answer it, Adèle. I 'm not at home to anyone.

ADÈLE

If it should be Mr. Lafont, ma'am?

CLOTILDE

I said I was not at home to anyone. That includes Mr. Lafont as well as anyone else.

ADÈLE

Yes, ma'am.

CLOTILDE

Leave the doors open so I can hear what is said. If it should be somebody wanting to see my husband, ask him to wait, and I 'll come out.

ADÈLE

I understand, ma'am. (*A third ring*) Yes, we 're very impatient, but it won't help much!

CLOTILDE

I ought to have hurried. I should have been on my
way by now, and then I would n't have been bothered.
(*Going to the rear door, which she holds ajar*) It 's
him, sure enough. He could n't miss such a fine
chance. . . . Come, speak up, why don't you?
That 's right; question the servant! I think he 's
asking Adèle where I am. . . . He 's insisting. . . .
What? Adèle is letting him in! (*Returning to the
front of the stage, slowly*) My goodness, he 's coming in, he 's coming in! Is he going to wait here?
Oh, these men! When we don't care for them any
longer, how they do run after us! (*She goes quickly
to the right and hides behind the door, where she can
watch what happens on the stage*)

LAFONT (*entering*)

All right, my girl, all right.

ADÈLE

Why don't you take my word for it, sir? You can
see there 's no one here.

LAFONT

I 'll wait.

ADÈLE

Wait for whom? My mister and mistress have both
gone out.

LAFONT (*hesitating*)

Together?

ADÈLE

No, sir, not together. He went out alone, and so
did she.

LAFONT

Did Mr. Du Mesnil say when he would be back?

ADÈLE

> All I know is that Mrs. Du Mesnil is n't coming back. She 's going to dine in town.

LAFONT (*after some hesitation*)

> With Mr. Du Mesnil?

ADÈLE

> No, sir.   They are going to dine separately.

LAFONT

> You can go on with your work, my girl.   I see some writing materials here; I 'll leave a little note.

ADÈLE

> As you please, sir.   I 'm not the boss here.   I can't show you the door. (*She goes out*)

LAFONT (*not aware of Clotilde, who is still hiding behind the door at the right*)   I 'm here.   I don't know why I 'm here, though.   I 've put my foot in it again. . . . I 've got to cool off and make up my mind to a separation that has become necessary. . . . In Paris you can't keep a semi-respectable mistress; it is n't possible.   The more respectable she is, the less chance you have of keeping her. . . . I 'm going to have an explanation with Clotilde . . . an explanation that will move heaven and earth!   It will be the graceful thing for me to do; and then I 'll break with her once and for all.   Here I 'm in a turmoil, running after her, looking for her this way while she is running that way . . . What 's the use?   What more do I need to know? . . . She is the mistress of that man Mercier; it 's as clear as daylight.   Since when?   What good would it do me to know? — And why?   That 's it; why?   I 'll be hanged if I can tell why!   Probably she does n't really care for him

— which would be some consolation. . . . What am I
going to do? If Adolph were only here, we might
spend the day together. It's the truth: I always
care more for the husband when I'm sick at heart;
and Clotilde has been standing me on my head. He
makes me feel less lonely. In Adolph's position there
is a certain consolation for my own — for his is
worse than mine — of course, it's worse! After all,
if Clotilde owes no respect to me, she's doing her
husband a very great wrong. . . . I'm capable of
judging her conduct severely, now that I find myself
in the same box with her husband. . . . What utter
loneliness! Here I am marooned all at once, with
nothing to cling to, sick at heart, confronted with
a disgusting situation, and getting farther into it
all the time! Say, but men have a hard time of it!
Either celibates or cuckolds — and between those two
states the choice is hardly worth while.

CLOTILDE (*coming forward*)

Well, I may as well come out. At any rate, I'll
know what he wants of me.

LAFONT

What! You here?

CLOTILDE

Well? What's strange about my being here? The
strange thing is your being here — you, whom I for-
bade the house — and in plain language, too. This
is the way you thank me for my forbearance! You
are constantly inventing new ways of displeasing
me, and I'm fool enough to forgive you every time.

LAFONT

It's your fault!

CLOTILDE

Oh, please don't begin again! No scenes to-day! I simply won't be dragged into one. Had you any reason — any pretext — some frightful discovery that you could n't keep to yourself any longer?

LAFONT

Really, I was afraid you were suffering.

CLOTILDE

That was very nice of you. Now you 've seen me, and reassured yourself — (*she points at the door, imitating with her hand the flight of a bird*) — fly away. (*A pause*)

LAFONT

Are you going out?

CLOTILDE

It looks like it, does n't it? As a rule I don't parade around my apartment with my hat on.

LAFONT

Are you in a hurry?

CLOTILDE

I 'm late now.

LAFONT

Let 's not make up our minds yet.

CLOTILDE

What do you mean by that?

LAFONT

I thought we might have dinner together; if I am still your old schoolmate.

CLOTILDE

There 's no longer any schoolmate — neither you nor anybody else. I 've come to the conclusion that these restaurant frolics have all kinds of disadvantages.

They lead me into lies I don't like to tell; and I
can't do so any more. . . . Am I not right?

LAFONT

Don't ask me what I think.

CLOTILDE

Do you want me to?

LAFONT

I am ready for anything after this.

CLOTILDE

That's always the wisest plan. Then you'll never
be disappointed.

LAFONT

Come, be nice now! Let's sit down and have a
friendly talk.

CLOTILDE

I have n't the time . . . to talk. Some other day
— to-morrow, if that'll suit you.

LAFONT

To-morrow I'd be waiting for you, and at the last
moment something else would turn up to keep you
from coming.

CLOTILDE

You don't want to-morrow? . . . Just as you please.
That suits me perfectly. I'm never anxious to be
with discontented, disagreeable people.

LAFONT

It's love that makes me so.

CLOTILDE (*pouting*)

Love is a bore.

LAFONT

Oh, please have pity on me; please! It's easy to
see you don't feel as I do. Here I'm in despair,
chilled to the heart, while you are gadding around.

CLOTILDE

Gadding! What kind of an expression do you call that? Admitting I am cold toward you — which is possible — do you think a woman can be won back by carrying on as you have been doing — harassing her all the time? It has the very opposite effect; she gets bored, and angry, and you put notions in her head that she would never have dreamed of otherwise. (*Approaching him with feigned tenderness that deceives him for the moment*) Take a little trip somewhere. (*Lafont starts*) Yes; take a little trip. Disappear . . . for six months — that would n't be so terrible. A separation would be just the thing at this time. When you came back, your disposition would be improved. You need n't be afraid on my account. I 'm not the kind of a woman that forgets things readily. You 'd find me just as I used to be. Don't you want to try it? No; you don't! You can't go away for six months when your mistress asks it as a favor; even though she would regard it as a real sign of your love. (*A pause*)

LAFONT

Where are you going?

CLOTILDE

Is that the only answer I get?

LAFONT

Where are you going?

CLOTILDE

I felt so sure you would ask that question that I 've been waiting for it ever since you came in!

LAFONT

Does it embarrass you?

CLOTILDE

Not in the least. You 'd be a good deal better off,
would n't you, when you knew where I was going?
And what 's to prevent my saying, " I 'm going
such and such a place " — and then I might go somewhere else?

LAFONT

I 'd follow you.

CLOTILDE

Follow me? I dare you to! Much good it has done
you so far. Be careful. I am fond of you —
really fond of you. I make allowances for everything; for the condition you are in, and for the
moments we have spent together: but you must n't
think you can take undue advantage of these things.
(*Pointedly*) I do as I choose; and it concerns nobody but my husband.

LAFONT

You 're deceiving me!

CLOTILDE

I? . . . With whom? . . . Who? . . . Who? . . .
You 'd better learn that suspicions are n't enough,
when you accuse a woman. You 've got to have the
proof. When there is proof, and a woman is really
guilty, a real man knows what he has to do; he has
to leave her . . . or keep still.

LAFONT

Clotilde!

CLOTILDE

Who? . . . Tell his name, if you know it! I 'd like
to know the name of this Don Juan. Perhaps I
weary him by running after him; and he does n't
think himself so very lucky! . . . You 're forcing me

to tell you something I wanted to keep from you.
I 've done a terribly wrong thing! I had a husband,
and children, and a cosey little home; and I wanted
more; I wanted everything. Like all women, I have
had dreams about an ideal life, in which I could do
my duty without giving all my love — a combination
of heaven and earth! It was your fate to be the one
to show me how impossible it is. I don't know how
another woman might have succeeded; there 's nothing in it for me. I 've done it, it can't be helped now;
but it will be the first and last time. (*She takes out
her handkerchief and puts it to her eyes with a slight
show of emotion*)

LAFONT

You 're suffering!

CLOTILDE (*sitting down*)

It 's nothing! It will pass!

LAFONT

I was wrong.

CLOTILDE (*with deep feeling*)

Very wrong.

LAFONT

I 'll go.

CLOTILDE

That 's what you 'd better do.

LAFONT (*walking away and then returning*)

Forget what I said. I did n't mean anything by it.
I don't really believe you are deceiving me. You are
too good — too sincere. You appreciate, deep down
in your heart, my affection for you. I thought you
were waiting for me, and that we would have our
regular holiday — as we have been wont. When
you said " No " I lost my temper. Where are you

going? Visiting? Looking up some woman friend?
Is it a pleasure trip; or some absolute necessity?
Call it off, if you have to. Write and say your husband is sick and you must stay with him; that's
simple enough. Do what I ask you. Give me this
day. It has been mine for a long time; you've kept
it for me till now.

CLOTILDE

I'd like to, but I can't.

LAFONT

Why not?

CLOTILDE

They'll come for me with a carriage to take me to
the Park.

LAFONT

You were going out.

CLOTILDE

You're mistaken. I was waiting.

LAFONT

Mrs. Simpson?

CLOTILDE

That's just who . . . I'm going to dine with her.
(*Rising*) What a queer man you are! You take
offence at everything, even things that ought to cheer
you up.

LAFONT

Mrs. Simpson!

CLOTILDE

Of course, I forgot that Mrs. Simpson was not one of
your friends, and that you had forbidden me to go
to her house. A delightful house, magnificently furnished and perfectly irreproachable! Perhaps there

are a few little love-affairs going on — I would n't
deny it — but that's the same everywhere.

LAFONT

You know very well that Mrs. Simpson has a pretty
bad reputation.

CLOTILDE

So much the worse for those who have been the cause
of it! When a man has been intimate with a woman
that woman ought to be sacred for him — yes
sacred! That's a principle you should bear in mind
it may be of service to you. . . . I'm getting fright
ened, I confess. I can't help wondering what we are
coming to — what you've still got up your sleeve
To-day you have offered me the worst insult a woman
can hear. What else? What more are you going to
do? The only thing I can think of is violence. I
hope you'll control yourself and at least not go that
far. Consider well, my friend: it would be much
better that we separated right now if you think you
might be carried that far. Come now, I'm sending
you away in earnest this time. Your mind is easy
now, is n't it? In spite of the horror you have of
Mrs. Simpson, you would rather have me with her
. . . The first time I see you, we'll take up that mat
ter of the six-months' trip, and I'll persuade you to
take it, I hope.

LAFONT (*piteously*)

To-morrow?

CLOTILDE

Oh, to-morrow! It's different now, is it? So you do
want to see me to-morrow? Well, all right. There's
only one answer. But take care what you do. You
are calm and collected enough just now; don't

change the minute you get outside the door. You 're
on dangerous ground, I want to tell you. If you
should bother me between now and to-morrow — if I
just meet you . . . in the Park or anywhere else —
if you just show your nose anywhere, you won't see
me again as long as you live.

LAFONT

To-morrow, then?

CLOTILDE

To-morrow. (*He goes out quickly*) Well, there was
nothing else I could say. He was sensible enough.
I like it when he gets angry, but I 'm always afraid
he 's going to cry. (*Going to the window*) I 'd better make sure before I go downstairs that I have n't
got him behind me. There he goes, dejectedly, with
his head down. Poor fellow! Oh, I 'll pay him a
little visit to-morrow, of course. What 's the matter
with him now? He 's stopped. He 's coming back.
He 's coming right into the house. Oh, the villain!
He 's going to lie in wait for me and wear me out.
I 'm going to let him know I see him; it 's the only
way I can get out of here.
[*Du Mesnil enters at the rear door. He wears the
air of a man thoroughly disappointed and discouraged; he throws his hat on the table and sits down
near the table, after giving it an angry shove.*

CLOTILDE (*turning round and perceiving her husband*)
Now it 's the other one! (*Looking him over*) Adolph!
Adolph! What 's the matter with you? (*Going over
to him*) Adolph! Answer me!

DU MESNIL (*bitterly*)
Let me alone, will you?

CLOTILDE

What 's the trouble?   That 's a pretty face to show
when you get home!   I never saw you look like that
before!

DU MESNIL

Don't make me feel worse.   I don't feel like laughing, or listening to your chatter.

CLOTILDE (*uneasily, with a change of tone*)

What 's the matter?

DU MESNIL

You 'll know what it is — you 'll know it all too soon.

CLOTILDE

So it 's something serious?

DU MESNIL

Very serious.

CLOTILDE

You 're angry?

DU MESNIL

I 've got reason to be.

CLOTILDE

You 're angry . . . with me?

DU MESNIL

It 's nothing to do with you.   If you 're going out,
go ahead.   Go out!   (*She takes a few steps toward
the door*)   Where are you going, anyway?

CLOTILDE (*returning*)

To one of the big stores.

DU MESNIL

Go on, go to your big store.   Buy some of your fol-
derols.   It 's just the time for it.

CLOTILDE

I 'm getting tired of this.   I won't move a step till
you 've explained.   (*She tears off her hat*)   I 'm not

going out while my husband is in trouble, and I don't
know what the trouble is. (*Sitting down*) If he
won't tell me till he gets ready, I 'll wait.

DU MESNIL (*rising and going over to her*)
You 're mighty nice.

CLOTILDE
Well, speak out, then, you old goose.

DU MESNIL
We 're down and out.

CLOTILDE
How so?

DU MESNIL
How? About that collectorship.

CLOTILDE (*rising*)
Oh, that! What, you, a man — you get into such
a state of mind, and upset me like that, simply because there has been a hitch in a matter of that kind?
Why, there has been a hitch — that 's all! It 's what
always happens in such matters. One loses — the
other wins: and all you can do is to profit by your
gains and forget the losses. Did you think I was
going to complain, and have a lot of reproaches for
you? Never, my dear boy, never! Come, now —
brace up — and don't look so forlorn! What would
you do if you had a real run of bad luck? If you
should lose me, for instance? . . . And now which
one of us was right? That uncle of yours — a fine
kind of protector you 've got there! Nothing about
you ever pleased him: neither your way of living,
nor your writings, nor your wife. And then, whenever he mixes into anything, you can be sure it will
be a fizzle. How did he get into the Academy, any-

way? If he were n't a bachelor, I might guess. . . .
Tell me what happened. I don't know yet.

DU MESNIL

I don't know either.

CLOTILDE

It 's all settled, is it?

DU MESNIL

Almost.

CLOTILDE

Oh, is that all? What do you mean by " almost "?
Has the job been given out or not?

DU MESNIL

Not yet.

CLOTILDE

There 's nothing actually settled then?

DU MESNIL

The collectorship is about to be disposed of, and
I 've been given to understand that it 's not for me.

CLOTILDE

All right. Now we 're getting to the point. And
who has been picked in your place?

DU MESNIL (*having thrown up his hands*)

A . . . very commonplace fellow!

CLOTILDE

I don't doubt it. Married?

DU MESNIL

What 's that got to do with it?

CLOTILDE

Answer just the same.

DU MESNIL

Yes, married.

CLOTILDE

His wife is young?

DU MESNIL
About your age.

CLOTILDE
Pretty?

DU MESNIL
Attractive.

CLOTILDE (*in a lower tone*)
Giddy?

DU MESNIL
So they say.

CLOTILDE
Oh, the hussy!

DU MESNIL
I see what you've got in mind.

CLOTILDE
It's time you did.

DU MESNIL
You're mistaken. Those things don't work in the Treasury department.

CLOTILDE
Well, to sum it up: nobody has got the place yet, and you have let yourself become discouraged too easily — as your habit is.

DU MESNIL
All right! Let it go at that! But what is there to do?

CLOTILDE (*after reflection*)
Get out of my way. (*She passes abruptly in front of him, sits down at the table and begins to write*)

DU MESNIL
Just tell me.

CLOTILDE
Don't bother me.

DU MESNIL

Let's talk it over first.

CLOTILDE

No use. . . . I'm writing to Lolotte, to ask her to meet me somewhere; she'll understand that it's about something important.

DU MESNIL

Lolotte? Who the devil is Lolotte?

CLOTILDE

Lolotte is Mrs. Simpson. We call her Lolotte for short ever since she took that part in a play. And she likes it.

DU MESNIL

All right. Write to Lolotte. Say what you please. If Lolotte succeeds where a member of the Academy has fallen down, it will suit me all right, but I shall feel sorry for France.

CLOTILDE

Let France alone. France doesn't worry about you; so don't you worry about France. (*Rising*) Haven't you got something to do?

DU MESNIL

I made up my mind to come home and lock myself in for a week.

CLOTILDE

I don't want you to. I don't want you to make yourself sick about a thing that may come out all right yet. You can take this letter to Mrs. Simpson; that'll give you an airing. From there you can go and see your uncle.

DU MESNIL

Why? A fellow who is good for nothing, as you have just said yourself. I'm going to write him that

I 've got enough of his advice, and he can bestow his influence somewhere else.

CLOTILDE

Don't you do it. People know that your uncle has been trying to work you into this job; and whatever we get, it will be due to his influence; see? You don't want people saying that you are a protégé of Mrs. Simpson; and that we owe what we get to her and her friends.

DU MESNIL

You 're dead right. I 'll take this letter and then go and see my uncle. But the Economist Club will have to get along without me this time.

CLOTILDE

Not a bit of it. Why should you change your habits? You get a lot of fun out of those dinners. You get home late, with your chest puffed out, and with a lot of stories that give me a pretty good idea of what you are talking about most of the time. You are among a lot of men, and you say a lot of silly things; but you 're happy. Why deprive yourself of a little pleasure? There is n't too much of it in this world. You 'll be with the kind of men you like, and I 'll go to my friend, who 's distressed because she has n't seen me.

DU MESNIL

All right. Just as you say. But I 'm in low spirits to-day, and I 'd rather stay with you.

CLOTILDE

Thanks. But run along now, and don't mope. You 'll soon be yourself again.

DU MESNIL

Well, so long; I 'll deliver that letter of yours.

CLOTILDE

Good! (*He goes toward the door downheartedly*)
Throw your shoulders back, why don't you; and put
on as happy a look as you can. Don't let others see
that you have troubles — it does n't pay!

DU MESNIL (*returning*)

What shall I say to my uncle?

CLOTILDE

What you please.

DU MESNIL

Well, I want it understood that you 're sending me to
this dinner. And you 're sending me when I 'm in
a rotten state of mind.

CLOTILDE

That 'll pass away . . . when you get your feet under the table.

DU MESNIL

I 'm going to throw myself right into the midst of it.
(*He goes out*)

CLOTILDE

Just like a chapter of *Madame Bovary!* Talk about
a woman's cleverness and management! While she 's
in the house, the house prospers, I warrant you.
What would my husband do if he did n't have me?
Decent folks have a little luck, and people are well
disposed toward them; but whenever there 's something to be given out, how does it go? Whether it 's
a position, or a prize, or a favor, big or little, and
there are two candidates — one a worthy man, not
very strong, but modest and deserving — and the
other some humbug who has nothing but his wits;
it 's the humbug that gets the prize every time, and

the good man that gets it in the neck! Perhaps I'll
be able to leave the house some time to-day! I hope
Mr. Lafont has got tired of hanging around. He
can't kick this time, if I get the start of him. I'm
off! (*She goes rapidly toward the door; the door
opens slowly and furtively; Lafont hesitatingly shows
himself*) Oh, this is too much!

[*Clotilde returns to the front of the stage in a hurry;
furious with silent anger; like a woman resolved not
to say a single word.*

LAFONT

You're angry because I'm back again? . . . Here's
just how it happened. I was going away — honestly,
I was. I was n't going to think of you any more till
to-morrow. Well, I saw your husband coming home;
what could I do? . . . I would have been glad to
shake hands with him, but I thought perhaps you
did n't want him to know I had been here, so it was
better for me not to let him see me. . . . You always
tell me I don't know what I'm about when I'm
spending my time with Adolph for the sake of appearances. . . . So I came back in a hurry when
your husband was n't looking and dodged under a
shelter to let him go by. . . . He did come in, did n't
he? You must have seen him? I have n't been seeing a ghost, have I? . . . After that I showed some
weakness, I admit. I could n't stay there. I said
to myself: Clotilde has been waiting quite awhile
for Mrs. Simpson, and it does n't look very much
as though anybody were coming; so her plans must
have fallen through, and perhaps she'll be glad to
see me. Surely you are not going to find fault with
me on account of an idea that was both tender and

unassuming? . . . Well, your husband went out; but
that made no difference, because he did n't count, anyway. Then I looked again to see whether Mrs. Simpson's carriage was coming. I did n't see it, so I
came upstairs. Oh, really, I came up the stairs
trembling, and perhaps I 'd have gone down again
(*laughing*) if it had n't been for one of those lucky
shots — are n't they funny, though? — your husband left the door open. Come now, Clotilde, it 's
all simple and natural enough; don't be angry about
a little thing like that . . . say something. Don't
you want to? Not a single word? Just one. . . .
(*Going away*) All right; I 'll go. You certainly do
want this day to yourself. Till to-morrow then.
(*Returning*) To-morrow? (*Growing impatient*) Say
something! Don't you want to speak to me? (*Going
away*) I 'm hurt, I really am. You 've been treating me altogether too flippantly lately. You don't
give any thought to what has passed between us.
(*Returning*) You 've made up your mind not to
speak to me, have you? (*Going away*) Well, just as
you say; we 'll make an end of it. You don't love
me any longer. I 'm in your way. The pleasure I
get out of your company is not so great that I
could n't enjoy myself just as much somewhere else.
Let 's part! (*Returning to her and holding out his
hand*) Let 's part like good sports! . . . Do you
want me to tell you something? You were not
expecting anybody. You were going to visit your
lover; you were going to dinner with him; can you
deny it? . . . I know who he is; I did n't want to
mention his name before. His name — is — Ernest
Mercier.

CLOTILDE

Alfred Mercier.

LAFONT

Alfred?

CLOTILDE

Alfred Mercier.

LAFONT

Number 28 Madeleine Street.

CLOTILDE

Number 28 Madeleine Avenue.

LAFONT (*perplexed*)

Clotilde! Is this a joke, or are you telling me the truth? . . . It's the truth, is it? . . . (*Weeping*) Oh, Clotilde! Clotilde! What have you done? You ought to have deceived me delicately; without telling me, or letting me find it out. This is the end! This time, it's the end! Good-bye. (*Stopping*) Is it good-bye? . . . Good-bye! (*He goes out*)

CLOTILDE

Well; that's over with! I would have liked to be more obliging, and make some sort of explanation. But day after day — and twice a day! No, sir! A fine time a woman would have, with such explosions as those! She would n't have time to breathe! To say nothing about always being within a hair's breadth of a catastrophe! Really, I can never be at peace except when my husband is at home.

CURTAIN

THE THIRD ACT

The scene is the same as in the first and second acts. The double door at the right is wide open; the table has been placed in the centre of the room for serving coffee.

CLOTILDE (*near the table*)

Mr. Simpson . . .

SIMPSON (*seated and just finishing a cup of coffee*)

Yes, ma'am?

CLOTILDE

You 'll do just as you would at your mother's house, won't you? Help yourself.

SIMPSON

Yes, ma'am.

CLOTILDE (*giving a cup to Adèle*)

Give this cup to the gentleman, and then you may go.

ADÈLE

You don't need me any longer, ma'am?

CLOTILDE

No.

ADÈLE

I told you before, ma'am, that my brother . . .

CLOTILDE

Run along, now; you can talk to me about that later.

ADÈLE (*sourly*)

Very well, ma'am. (*She goes out at the right, carrying the cup*)

CLOTILDE (*drawing slowly near to Simpson, and speaking in a low tone*) So it's really true you are going to leave Paris?

SIMPSON

It's really true.

CLOTILDE

This very day?

SIMPSON

I take the seven o'clock train, which will bring me home at midnight.

CLOTILDE

Your trunks are packed?

SIMPSON

My servant is finishing them right now.

CLOTILDE

Is there nothing I can do for you?

SIMPSON

There's really so little time left; and I'm afraid of bothering you.

CLOTILDE

Just as you say. (*She leaves him; he rises and puts his cup on the table*) What does your mother think of this sudden determination?

SIMPSON

My mother is delighted to see me go. It's partly for her sake that I'm going sooner than usual. She wanted me to inspect the place from cellar to roof-tree and look after the necessary repairs. I want to make it impossible for my mother to recognize Croquignole when she goes back there to live.

CLOTILDE

If your mother agrees to your going, I 've nothing more to say.

SIMPSON

You 're too fond of Paris. You don't admit that anyone may find it irksome, or prefer to live anywhere else.

CLOTILDE

That 's not what I think. I only think that a man of your age and situated as you are would not be likely to leave Paris voluntarily, especially if there were some little affair of the heart to hold him. The winter is scarcely over. The weather is frightful. Nobody thinks of leaving except you. There must be a reason.

SIMPSON

There would rather be a reason for my staying.

CLOTILDE

Then why are you going away?

SIMPSON

I 'm being bored. I feel annoyed and humiliated. I cut a sorry figure in this Paris of yours. How about that dingy ground-floor apartment where I live? I 'm ashamed to live in it; and still more ashamed when anyone pays me a visit there. My mother still refuses to set me up in the style I desire. She prefers me to travel. I spend a lot of money, without getting either pleasure or glory out of it. It 's different over there in Croquignole. There I can make a showing. I amount to something when I 'm in the country; they bow to me when I pass by. I have everything I don't have here: horses — dogs — guns. You know I have a splendid collection of

guns; and I 'm worried about not finding them in
good condition when I get back. Paris is certainly a
nice place; I 'd have as good a time here as anybody if the conditions were such as to satisfy my
pride.

CLOTILDE

It 's my fault. I ought to have been more to you
and looked out for you better. To think of sepa-
rating as we are doing, light-heartedly, after only
four months! I hope the time has n't seemed long
to you.

SIMPSON

Five months.

CLOTILDE

Do you think so?

SIMPSON

Count them: 15th of January, 15th of February,
15th of March. . . .

CLOTILDE

You 're right. Call it five months and let it go at
that. (*A pause*)

SIMPSON (*coming near her*)

This year you ought to come to Croquignole when
my mother is there with a number of her society
people.

CLOTILDE

Don't expect me. My husband can't get away so
easily.

SIMPSON

Let him stay here.

CLOTILDE

He does n't like that.

SIMPSON

You 'd find your friend Mrs. Beaulieu there; she does n't let a little thing like that stop her from going.

CLOTILDE

Oh, Pauline! That 's different. In the first place she has money of her own, and can do as she pleases. And then, her husband behaved badly to her, and she takes advantage of that fact — and she is right, too.

SIMPSON

Mrs. Beaulieu has a pretty good time, does n't she?

CLOTILDE

I don't know anything about that. I 'm very close to Pauline, very; but we don't tell each other everything.

SIMPSON

She 's the one, though, that introduced you to my mother.

CLOTILDE

Pauline never knew why I wanted her to. What makes you think Mrs. Beaulieu does n't act just as she should? Has anybody been talking to you about her?

SIMPSON

I know of one wild infatuation, with one of my friends.

CLOTILDE

What 's his name?

SIMPSON

Hector de Godefroy.

CLOTILDE

That is n't true.

SIMPSON

It 's scarcely a secret.

CLOTILDE

Mrs. Beaulieu, as you ought to know, is in love with
a fine young fellow who is crazy about her and is
always with her.

SIMPSON

Who is that?

CLOTILDE (*hesitating, and with a smile*)

Alfred Mercier.

SIMPSON

Yes; but Mrs. Beaulieu is head over heels in love
with my friend Hector — I don't know why. She
does n't let a day pass without seeing him.

CLOTILDE

Where did you hear this?

SIMPSON

From Mrs. Beaulieu herself. She never hesitates to
tell things like that.

CLOTILDE

What a child Pauline is! She can't keep anything
to herself.

SIMPSON (*walking away*)

That 's another thing I like about getting away from
Paris. It rids one of a lot of rather shady stories.

CLOTILDE

You include my friend when you say that?

SIMPSON

I think it applies to her.

CLOTILDE

Pauline has had a good deal of trouble; remember
that.

SIMPSON

She does n't seem to have any nowadays.

CLOTILDE

Perhaps you 've been paying court there yourself.

SIMPSON

Never had the least idea of it.

CLOTILDE

Mrs. Beaulieu is a perfect dear, though.

SIMPSON

I don't like to be mixed up with a crowd.

CLOTILDE

But you must expect to be, sometimes.

SIMPSON

The ladies would n't like to hear you say that.

CLOTILDE

And what does it prove? That we are weak, fickle,
culpable, if you please; that we are forever getting
involved in love-affairs; that we meet a lot of boors
who don't love as we want to be loved; or, worse
still, thankless men who respect and love nobody but
themselves! However, you 're right, after all. The
wisest plan for us is to look at all men alike; to close
our eyes tight; to stop up our ears, and say to
ourselves bravely, " Your place is there; stay there."
Perhaps life would n't be so interesting or thrilling,
but we should avoid turmoil, and disillusionments,
and regrets.

SIMPSON

Why, what 's the matter?

CLOTILDE

Let me alone.

SIMPSON

Tears?

CLOTILDE

Yes; and honest ones, too.

SIMPSON

Why are you crying, dear?

CLOTILDE

How can I tell? There's a little of everything in a woman's tears.

SIMPSON

I'm awfully sorry my going away . . .

CLOTILDE

No. Don't make yourself out more responsible than you are. It's the old story: people come together, like each other, and then part. But you men are very free and easy before you get into our good graces, and mighty Puritanical afterwards. Come! I must call my husband now. He'd let us alone till to-morrow; he has such perfect faith and sublime ignorance of the way we carry on. It was you that got us what we wanted; but you did it after you and I had already loved each other; it was n't necessary. Some day, when you are coming this way again, if you feel like shaking hands, don't forget the house where there are so many reasons for your being welcome.

SIMPSON

You're charming!

CLOTILDE

I know it. (*She leaves him and goes to the door at the right*) Come, Adolph, you've smoked enough. You can finish the newspaper another time. Adolph, do you hear me? Mr. Simpson is ready to leave; get up immediately, if you're going with him! (*Returning*) He's coming.

DU MESNIL (*entering and approaching Simpson*)

I fear you 'll think me rude in deserting you like this.

SIMPSON

That 's all right.

DU MESNIL

It 's a habit of mine to take a few minutes' rest after luncheon; it 's the only time I feel really at home.

SIMPSON

Are you ready?

DU MESNIL

Whenever you are.

SIMPSON

Let 's be going, then.

DU MESNIL

Just let me say a word to my wife, will you?

SIMPSON

Certainly.

DU MESNIL (*going over to Clotilde and speaking in a low tone*) Ought I to thank this young man?

CLOTILDE

No; we invited him to luncheon; that 's enough.

DU MESNIL

We 're under great obligations to that friend of his that 's a friend of the Minister.

CLOTILDE

It was his mother who did everything . . . you remember when I wrote that letter to her — you were here?

DU MESNIL

I did n't know Mrs. Simpson had a son as old as that. What do you think of him?

CLOTILDE

A gentleman.

DU MESNIL
  Rather stuck-up, is n't he?

CLOTILDE
  That does n't offend me at all.

DU MESNIL
  What did he have to say to **you**?

CLOTILDE
  That I was perfect.

DU MESNIL
  Mentally.

CLOTILDE
  Physically, too.

DU MESNIL
  I 'm a pretty good sport to let you two be together.

CLOTILDE
  He 's leaving to-night.

DU MESNIL
  He might come back, though.

CLOTILDE (*in her husband's ear*)
  It would take more than him to make me forget my
  duty.

SIMPSON (*going over to Clotilde*)
  You 'll excuse me, Mrs. Du Mesnil, for leaving so
  soon.

CLOTILDE
  I know your time is valuable; you told me so, and
  I don't dare detain you.

SIMPSON
  I 'm already longing for Paris — before I leave.

CLOTILDE
  You can forget it easily enough.

SIMPSON

My mother will see you very soon, of course, and she will give me the news of you.

CLOTILDE

We shall want to hear about you, too.

SIMPSON

Remember, you 're expected at Croquignole.

CLOTILDE

It is n't likely you 'll see me there.

SIMPSON

I have n't given up hope yet. If there should be any occasion for me to come to Paris — and I 'll see that there is — I 'm going to try once more to persuade you.

CLOTILDE

Don't come to invite me — come to see me.

SIMPSON

So long, then.

CLOTILDE

So long.

[*Simpson leaves.*

DU MESNIL

What was it I was saying?

CLOTILDE

What was it I replied? Never mind, run along about your business. (*Du Mesnil goes out*) What a stupid adventure! The young men nowadays are n't worth the trouble they give you. They 're unfeeling, full of affectations; they don't believe in anything; they like to pose, and that 's all. I did think that Mr. Simpson, brought up by such a mother, would form a real attachment for a woman! However, I have n't any real complaint against him. He always acted

like a perfect gentleman and was very obliging. . . .
He made me a bit tired with his talk about his guns.
. . . It serves me right. I already had all I needed
— a good friend, a second husband, so to speak. I
abused him in every way I could think of. He got
enough of it at last, that's plain. Who knows?
Perhaps he thought I was angrier than I really was.
Men know women so little. It's true we are very
weak toward those we love, but in the end we always
get back to those who love us. (*The bell rings*)

ADÈLE (*entering*)

Mr. Lafont, ma'am.

CLOTILDE

Well? Why do you seem so astonished when you
announce Mr. Lafont?

ADÈLE

Are you going to receive him, ma'am?

CLOTILDE

Of course.

ADÈLE

Very well, ma'am.

CLOTILDE

You can run along, now, Adèle, if you must go out.

ADÈLE

Thank you, ma'am. (*She shows Lafont in*)

LAFONT (*slowly, with emotion*)

How do you do.

CLOTILDE (*with well-calculated voice*)

How do you do, my friend.

LAFONT

Do you feel well?

CLOTILDE

Nicely, very nicely. And you?

LAFONT

Badly. Miserably. Do I bother you?

CLOTILDE

Not in the least.

LAFONT

Perhaps you were going out?

CLOTILDE

Oh, no indeed. I hardly ever go out nowadays. Where should I go?

LAFONT

Did you have company at luncheon?

CLOTILDE

You 'd hardly say that; just one.

LAFONT

A friend?

CLOTILDE

An acquaintance.

LAFONT

Might I know his name?

CLOTILDE (*as though trying to recollect it*)

My husband told me, but I don't seem to recall.

LAFONT

I saw them go out together.

CLOTILDE

Indeed? So you were down below, with your eyes open? If I had known that, I would have shown myself for a moment. It was very nice of you. You did n't forget me right away, after all.

LAFONT

Who was that man?

CLOTILDE

An acquaintance, I told you. A mere acquaintance. He is n't dangerous to you. My husband introduced

him to me this morning and he's going away to-
night.

LAFONT

Are you telling me the truth?

CLOTILDE

Why should I lie to you now? You have n't changed
much, I must say! Come, sit down in the armchair
and stay there, if you can. I don't want to see you
pacing back and forth and getting in a state of
mind as you did before. I have better memories of
you than that.

LAFONT

Clotilde!

CLOTILDE

There's no more Clotilde for you.

LAFONT

Dearie!

CLOTILDE

A little calmer, please — then we won't make so many
mistakes.

LAFONT

Honestly, I've been very sorry about that silly
quarrel. But you could have put an end to it so
quickly, if you had wanted to! Look at me! Alfred
Mercier! (*She laughs*) Well, what do you expect?
I had been jealous of this man Mercier for a long
time. All my suspicions were fastened on him. Mrs.
Beaulieu ought to appreciate your discretion.

CLOTILDE

That's all right. What have you been doing since
I saw you last?

LAFONT

Thinking of you.

CLOTILDE

That goes without saying.   What else?

LAFONT

What else?   Just the same as usual.

CLOTILDE

You did n't go away?

LAFONT

That would have forced me to move, and I did n't
have the heart.

CLOTILDE

Have the ladies been kind to you?   Have you been
well taken care of?

LAFONT

I won't answer such a question.

CLOTILDE

Why not?   In the old days I might possibly have
taken your infidelity to heart — very much to heart.
But what was forbidden you then, you are wholly
free to do now.   After all, I don't really know you
— whether you are the kind of a man to deprive
yourself of consolations.   You 're not always very
nice, nor jolly, and you 're suspicious, too — but —

LAFONT

But —

CLOTILDE

We won't talk about those things.

LAFONT

I was wounded too deeply, really, to dream of
consolations.   Besides, if my misfortune should have
caused me to lose you forever, I should never try to
find a substitute in those circles I have ceased to
frequent.

CLOTILDE

You 're wrong. You ought to go back to those women. They 're free to do as they please. They like trumped-up yarns, and squabbles and scraps. You 'll never get those things with me. All I have to offer is a peaceful, sincere love — without expecting anything for it.

LAFONT

That 's what I want. That 's what we all want.

CLOTILDE

Then you must be careful, and not risk all you have for the pleasure of flying into a passion.

LAFONT

Clotilde!

CLOTILDE

What is it?

LAFONT

Give me your hand.

CLOTILDE

No.

LAFONT

Surely you can give me your hand.

CLOTILDE

We 'll see, later on. Now don't look that way, or I 'll send you away this minute.

LAFONT

Give me your hand.

CLOTILDE

Well, there it is. Now I suppose you 'll have to have the other one.

LAFONT

You 're awfully cold toward me.

CLOTILDE

What, cold? I let you sit near me, and permit you to
hold my hands — did you think I was going to throw
my arms around your neck the minute you came in?

LAFONT

Here I am, a culprit. Heap the reproaches on my
head. I 'll take them. But I think you deserve
some, too.

CLOTILDE

No, sir.

LAFONT

Was it my fault or yours that our relations changed
so suddenly? There was n't a happier man than I
until you began to turn your whole existence upside
down.

CLOTILDE

What 's that? I began to turn it? No, that 's what
you would have done, if I had n't stopped you in
time.

LAFONT

You 're right. I don't know why I came back to
that. Let bygones be bygones.

CLOTILDE

What bygones? You 're simply incorrigible. I let
you call, and listen to you, and begin to believe sincerely that you 're sorry for your strange conduct.
And then I tell myself that if you were really to re-
form, it is barely possible that I might forgive you
— and then you make me angry again with that
contrariness of yours. I detest that spirit in you.
I 've never succeeded in conquering it. There are
no bygones, understand? Not a thing — nothing,

nothing, nothing — absolutely nothing!   Get away
from me!

LAFONT

Why?

CLOTILDE

Get away.   I want to get up.

LAFONT

No.

CLOTILDE

Yes.

LAFONT

Let 's stay as we are.

CLOTILDE

Let me get up a minute. . . . You need n't go
yet. . . .

LAFONT

No, let 's stay as we are.

CLOTILDE

What insistence!

LAFONT

You 're not in pain?

CLOTILDE

I 'm nervous and excited.

LAFONT

All the more reason . . .

CLOTILDE

What 's that?

LAFONT

I 'm hardly able to control myself, either.

CLOTILDE

Well, don't trouble yourself; I 'll stay here.

LAFONT

So you were thinking a little bit about forgiving me?

CLOTILDE

That 's what I said. But I was wrong.

LAFONT

Let 's take up our old relations where we left off.

CLOTILDE

What 's the use? You 'll never be happy with me
nor I with you. You don't want to take the trouble
to understand my position.

LAFONT

What position?

CLOTILDE

My position. Am I not married? Am I not entirely
dependent on my husband, who has the right to find
me here whenever he wants me? You 'll admit that '
the least he can ask. Then there 's another grave
fault; and you 'd avoid it, if you knew me better.

LAFONT

What 's this new reproach?

CLOTILDE

You don't like my husband.

LAFONT

Yes, I do, really.

CLOTILDE

No, you don't, really. You don't like Adolph. You
show it in a number of ways. Perhaps it 's because
your characters are not suited; or maybe it 's my
position that causes it.

LAFONT

How unjust! Your husband? He never had but
two real friends in this world.

CLOTILDE

Two?

LAFONT

Yes; two.

CLOTILDE

What two?

LAFONT

You and I. (*They laugh*) But let's leave others aside and talk about ourselves. Come now, Clotilde, be honest: is it a fact that I like you?

CLOTILDE

Why, yes. I think I suit your taste pretty well.

LAFONT

You don't run across a love like mine every day — you realize that, don't you?

CLOTILDE

Certainly. It's just because I realize it and feel it deeply that I've put up with all your brain-storms.

LAFONT

I'm usually very affectionate, very loving. . . .

CLOTILDE

I don't deny it. You know perfectly how to be nice when you want to be, and you say a lot of things that are very pleasant to hear. . . . You don't talk about guns.

LAFONT

What do you mean by that?

CLOTILDE

Oh, nothing. A silly story I heard. Never mind!

LAFONT (*coming near her again*)

Tell me you forgive me.

CLOTILDE (*in a low voice*)

Yes . . . now be sensible, won't you?

LAFONT

You forgive me . . . everything?

CLOTILDE

Everything. . . . Don't plague me again, and I 'll come to see you.

LAFONT

Very soon?

CLOTILDE

Whenever you like. . . . Be careful; I 'm not alone in the house.

LAFONT

Clotilde!

CLOTILDE

Do you love me?

LAFONT

I worship you.

CLOTILDE (*rising*)

Here we 've said a lot of useless words, all to get back to the same point.

LAFONT (*going toward her*)

Do you regret it?

CLOTILDE

Not now.

LAFONT

I was very miserable when I came here. I 'm leaving in the highest spirits.

CLOTILDE

Well, I hope you 'll profit by this experience. No more scenes, understand? No more of those awful suspicions. Women don't like them, and they 're useless. When things are going badly, or you feel out of sorts about something, tell me. I 'm always ready to listen to reason. Now listen. I 'm going to tell you a piece of news you 'll like.

LAFONT

I 'm all ear.

CLOTILDE

I believe my intimacy with Mrs. Simpson is over with.

LAFONT

You don't say!

CLOTILDE

Yes.

LAFONT

Have you had a quarrel with her?

CLOTILDE

No. On the contrary, I 've nothing but praise for her. It is n't exactly Mrs. Simpson I don't want to see any more; I just think it 's better not to go to her house.

LAFONT

What did I tell you a short time ago!

CLOTILDE

Well, you 've got more shrewdness than I, that 's all.

LAFONT

I know someone else you ought not to go with. You 'd do well to cut her out, too.

CLOTILDE

Now you 're going to say something foolish; I can see it coming. This someone else is . . .

LAFONT

Mrs. Beaulieu.

CLOTILDE

What, break with Pauline? I 'd like to know why. Why?

LAFONT

It seems to me . . .

CLOTILDE

What seems to you?

LAFONT

Mr. Mercier!

CLOTILDE

Well? Mr. Mercier?

LAFONT

I 've found out what he is to her. And you know well enough, too.

CLOTILDE

Yes, I do know. What of it?

LAFONT

I don't suppose you 'd defend her conduct, would you?

CLOTILDE

Oh, come now! Just stop to think what you 're saying. Are you going to blame Pauline for being to Mr. Mercier what I am to you?

LAFONT

That 's altogether different.

CLOTILDE

Are you so sure? What 's the difference?

LAFONT

I see one.

CLOTILDE

What one? Come, speak up. What do you see? . . . You men are all alike. Where you 're concerned, anything goes; but you hold up your hands in horror when others do the same. Rather than bother your head about Pauline, you 'd better be thinking about my husband. He 's been complaining every day that he does n't see you any more. He wants to know the reason.

LAFONT (*pointing at the second rear door*)

  Was that Adolph that we just heard come in?

CLOTILDE

  Yes, that was Adolph. Have you thought of what
  you 're going to say to him?

LAFONT

  No.

CLOTILDE

  No? And that makes you laugh. All right for you,
  my friend. Get out of it as best you can.

DU MESNIL (*entering*)

  Well, lo and behold!

LAFONT (*embarrassed*)

  How are you, old chap?

DU MESNIL

  And how are you? Why have n't we seen you all this
  time?

LAFONT (*embarrassed*)

  How are you getting along?

DU MESNIL

  Fine as silk. You did n't answer my question.
  What 's happened that you have n't been showing up
  here at all?

CLOTILDE

  Don't tease him. He has a great sorrow, have n't
  you, Mr. Lafont?

LAFONT

  Yes, Mrs. Du Mesnil.

DU MESNIL

  What sorrow?

CLOTILDE

  Shall I tell my husband?

LAFONT

If you want to.

DU MESNIL

Let's have it.

CLOTILDE

He's been jealous.

DU MESNIL

Jealous! (*To Lafont*) What? You're still jealous, at your age? (*To his wife*) And who the devil is he jealous of? Some woman who does n't belong to him, I'll bet. These single men! They deny themselves nothing. And then they are jealous in the bargain. Want me to tell you a famous economist's definition of jealousy? Jealousy is being deprived of something one wants. That's all. If you were married, you would n't be deprived, and then you would n't be jealous. Is n't that right, Clotilde?

CLOTILDE

Now you had better stop!

DU MESNIL

Jealous! (*To his wife*) Did you tell him . . . ?

CLOTILDE

What?

DU MESNIL

That I got that appointment.

CLOTILDE

Mr. Lafont was the first one who wrote and congratulated you.

DU MESNIL

That's right. I did n't remember. He wrote me instead of coming to see me. . . . (*To Lafont, all the time looking intently at his wife*) It was my uncle, my good old uncle, who turned the trick.

CLOTILDE

Everybody knows it was your uncle. You don't have to shout it from the housetops.

DU MESNIL

Well, it 's better to be a revenue collector than to be jealous, eh? (*To his wife*) This poor Lafont! He is n't yet out of his sulks. His nose is n't back in joint yet. . . . Come now, did she deceive you, or did n't she?

LAFONT

Don't bother me.

DU MESNIL

You can tell an old pal like me. Did she or did n't she?

CLOTILDE

My husband is asking you a question. Why don't you answer?

LAFONT

What do you want me to say? Is there a man, any man, who can swear that his mistress has n't deceived him? Mine says no; she could n't very well say yes. We 've made up again; that 's of course what we both wanted.

CLOTILDE

Really! It 's a good thing the lady is n't here when you say that. She might guess what opinion you hold of her and other women. Faith, Mr. Lafont, absolute faith — that 's the only winning card with us.

DU MESNIL

It 's the one I have always played, dearest!

CURTAIN

THE MERRY–GO–ROUND

(LA NAVETTE)

A COMEDY IN ONE ACT

1878

PERSONS

Arthur
Alfred
Armand
Antonia
Adèle

THE MERRY-GO-ROUND

SCENE

The stage is set as a fashionable Parisian drawing-room. At the back is an entrance with double doors; two other entrances with single doors, one at the left in the foreground, the other at the right in the background. At the right, in the foreground, a sofa. At the left a table and writing materials. Other articles of furniture.

When the curtain rises, Antonia and Alfred are seated at a card table set in the centre of the stage.

ANTONIA

Forty bezique! Do you hear? I 've got forty bezique! Take a card. Take a card, will you! Now please play, or go away!

ALFRED (*throwing down his cards*)

You are right, Antonia; I 'll get out of here. (*He rises and goes to get his cane and hat; then returning to Antonia, who has also risen*) Antonia!

ANTONIA (*going in front of him and guiding him toward the door on the left*) Au revoir, my dear.

ALFRED

Where are you going?

ANTONIA

You can see, can't you? — I 'm going into my bed-room.

ALFRED

> Hang it all, wait a minute; I 'm going to leave.

ANTONIA (*halting*)

> Leave.

ALFRED (*after a display of bad humor, places his cane and hat on the card table and comes close to Antonia*)

> I don't understand you, Antonia, dear. I come here and you make a row; the quarrel annoys me, and you start a game of bezique; playing bezique bores me, and you pack me off.

ANTONIA

> It 's your fault. Why did you come so late, when I was n't expecting you?

ALFRED

> It strikes me, Antonia, that I have the right to come here at any time that suits me.

ANTONIA

> The right! The right! You never talk of anything but your right! I have n't made an agreement with you not to see anybody or not to go anywhere.

ALFRED

> Look at the way you treat me! You ask me to drop in at your dressmaker's. I go there like a good fellow, and I bring you her receipted bill. You scarcely give me a word of thanks for it.

ANTONIA

> What do I care for one little bill?

ALFRED

> Bear in mind that this attention was quite voluntary on my part. I was n't bound to do it, according to our little understanding.

ANTONIA

Our little understanding! You talk enough about our little understanding, so I am in no danger of forgetting it. I'm getting sick of it. Alfred gets up late in the morning! Alfred takes breakfast with his friends. He goes to the Stock Exchange, to his club, to the auction rooms; he goes everywhere, Alfred does; while I, his mistress, stay here and wait patiently for him to come. Have you bothered your head in the least with my business?

ALFRED

What business?

ANTONIA

Should n't you enquire at the Insurance Company . . . about that little annuity you've been promising me so long?

ALFRED

I've been at your dressmaker's.

ANTONIA

That is n't enough. You must go to the Insurance Company, too. Are you going?

ALFRED

I'm going when I get ready.

ANTONIA

Stay here then. (*She leaves him and goes out at the left*)

ALFRED

I've played the fool. I've certainly played the fool! My relations with Antonia used to be delightful. Antonia had a protector — who annoyed us a little — but nevertheless our relations were delightful. I wanted to be the protector myself. Why? That's it, why? It was a matter of maintaining my dignity.

In the long run a man gets tired of those three-cornered arrangements which demand on a woman's part such endless precaution, such an excessive delicacy — which she does n't always have. Besides, I wanted to make my friendship for Antonia place her in an exceptional position — somewhere between good society and bad — nearer to the good, if possible. For instance, Antonia and her mother had not seen each other for a long time, and my first thought was to have a reconciliation. Antonia and her mother can't remain together five minutes without pulling hair, but she is company for the little girl. I give Antonia her due. She really appreciates the honorable side of my conduct toward her; but on the money side she is n't satisfied. She is unreasonable. One day it is this thing, the next day something else. She does n't swindle me; no, the poor girl is incapable of swindling me. She — she's trimming me. That's the way to put it — she's trimming me. Well, I don't like it. It's annoying. After all, though, I realize that she is justified. She gave up a good position for me. She is young, pretty, faithful. Oh, she surely is faithful! Only yesterday she was saying to me, reminding me of the time when I was not the only one, " Not for the world, not for anything in the world, would I go back to such an existence."

[*Antonia reënters; Arthur is seen behind her holding her by the waist; she closes the door in his face.*

ANTONIA

What! I leave you here alone. You must see that I 've had enough of you for to-day. And now I come back and find you here?

ALFRED

You did n't think I would go away without saying good-bye? Antonia, tell me the meaning of this persistence in trying to get rid of me. It does n't deceive me. Are you going out?

ANTONIA

I am not going out.

ALFRED

Then you are expecting someone?

ANTONIA

I am expecting no one. It only remains for you to get suspicious of me and start a jealous quarrel. Take your hat, shake hands, and go away. We shall only be saying mean things again, and that 's of no use.

ALFRED (*obeying mechanically*)

When shall I see you again?

ANTONIA

Whenever you like.

[*He goes to the door at the back of the stage; Antonia accompanies him; he hesitates again for a moment and then goes out.*

ANTONIA

At last! He 's gone at last! (*Coming back to the front of the stage*) I used to be crazy about that fellow, and now I can't bear the sight of him. How changeable men are! (*Going to the door at the left and opening it*) Arthur! Arthur!

ARTHUR (*aside, after giving several indications of weariness and displeasure*) This state of affairs can't go on much longer!

ANTONIA

Now be nice, Arthur. Set that table back, gather up the cards and put them out of my sight. Hurry up!

ARTHUR (*obeying mechanically; aside*)

I do the housework — in the other fellow's house. (*He folds up the card table and puts it back in its place on the right side of the rear entrance*)

ANTONIA

Now come here to me. What are you thinking about?

ARTHUR

I am thinking of us — us three.

ANTONIA

The subject is n't agreeable, my dear.

ARTHUR

I don't find it agreeable, either. So this is what you call spending the day together — I in there, you out here — with the other man!

ANTONIA

The other man! The other man! Go ahead and pity yourself!

ARTHUR

What do you mean by that?

ANTONIA

Never mind. I know what I mean. Come here, you naughty creature. You don't deserve all the trouble that I go to for you. What kind of a face is that to make to your girlie? Smile a little — quick now! — Better than that! — That 's more like it!

ARTHUR

Do you love me, Antonia?

ANTONIA

Yes, I love you. If I did n't love you, why should I let you stay around here? It is n't because of anything you give me, is it?

ARTHUR

I was expecting that reproach.

ANTONIA

I don't say it as a reproach, my dear. If you have n't a cent, it is n't your fault.

ARTHUR

I have n't a cent!

ANTONIA

Everybody knows perfectly well that young men are not rolling in money. But I have seen very few as dead broke as you are.

ARTHUR

Broke! I am dead broke! (*Aside*) This state of things can't go on much longer. Antonia!

ANTONIA

Yes, dear?

ARTHUR

Antonia, who knows but that I might wake up to-morrow morning with a fortune?

ANTONIA

I don't say no. It takes so little nowadays to make a fortune — some good political graft would do it.

ARTHUR

An inheritance would do it, too.

ANTONIA

Oh, inheritances! You always have to wait a long time for those.

ARTHUR

Nevertheless, they come. Late, very much too late,
but yet they come. What would you think of an inheritance which might suddenly fall to me, and which
would be enough for two persons? What should we
do?

ANTONIA

That would depend on you.

ARTHUR

On me alone?

ANTONIA

What do you want me to say? What do you want
to know? Yes, boy, yes! If you could provide for
me properly, I should very quickly sacrifice my present position.

ARTHUR

Is that really so? You would sacrifice your position
for me?

ANTONIA

As quick as a wink.

ARTHUR

That's well enough to say.

ANTONIA

I'd do it, too. I don't want to grumble, Arthur,
but my life is n't one sweet song. I should love dearly
to live openly with you, all deception aside, without
that continual tyranny of " the other man," as you
call him — who is within his rights, after all, and
whom I cannot help pitying and respecting. My
dear, a hundred times I have been at the point of
sending him away. If I have n't done so, it was on
your account, solely on your account. I said to

myself: " Arthur is not rich, but he needs a little wealth around him; he likes my luxury, he gets the benefits of my worldly comforts." Perhaps you don't understand me, Arthur. It's only women that have such delicacy.

ARTHUR (*aside*)

This state of things can't go on much longer.

ANTONIA

My dear, we are talking a good deal without saying anything.

ARTHUR

Antonia, I see that you are not happy. You can't be happy. And as for me, I give you my word I suffer intensely, too.

ANTONIA

Pshaw!

ARTHUR

I have to shut my eyes on a lot of things. . . .

ANTONIA

What things?

ARTHUR

What things? Why, Antonia, when a man loves a woman it is n't very pleasant — *that,* for one thing, is n't very pleasant. I don't enjoy it any more, staying there in that room. . . .

ANTONIA

What difference do two or three hours make? You could put them in to much less advantage.

ARTHUR

It is n't the time I care for; it is the question of my dignity, if you want to know.

ANTONIA

Your dignity, my dear? Is that what worries you
so much?

ARTHUR

Be careful, Antonia, be careful. That is just as if
you had made up your mind to slight my dignity.
You love me — yes, you tell me so, and I believe
you; but you don't show enough consideration for
me.

ANTONIA

You big calf!

ARTHUR

No, you don't show enough regard for me. The
consideration you show is n't for me — it 's for the
other man.

ANTONIA

Well, my dear, I 've really got to have something
for him.

ARTHUR (*brusquely*)

Good-bye, Antonia.

ANTONIA (*surprised*)

Good-bye?

ARTHUR

This state of affairs can't go on much longer.

ANTONIA

Why not?

ARTHUR

In the first place, it is repulsive to you.

ANTONIA

I did n't say that.

ARTHUR

In the second place, it humiliates me.

ANTONIA

It's rather late to think of that.

ARTHUR

From this time forth I've got to have you all to myself, or not at all.

ANTONIA

Are you asking me to make a sacrifice?

ARTHUR

Yes — and no. Good-bye, Antonia.

ANTONIA

Very well; as you please. Good-bye, dear.

ARTHUR

Good-bye, Antonia. Either I must have you all to myself or not at all. (*He goes out quickly*)

ANTONIA

He's going! He's leaving me! Without warning, without reason, without regret! And just when I was so happy with him, just when I loved him more than ever! Why? Our relationship is nothing new. We have both laughed over it many times. He had something on his mind he did n't tell me — there's no doubt about that. Oh, Arthur, Arthur! That is no way to treat a woman! If she does wrong, you can scold her. If she does it again, you can slap her. But it is n't right to leave her in the lurch. Such a fine fellow, so good-natured, full of fun — chuck full of fun. I was never bored one minute with that little rascal.

ADÈLE (*entering by the door on the right*)

Here are two letters for you, ma'am. One of them perhaps I should n't have taken. The other just came by messenger.

ANTONIA

Put the letters in your pocket. I'll read them next week.

ADÈLE

The messenger is waiting outside for an answer, ma'am. He said this one was from Mr. Delaunay.

ANTONIA (*surprised*)

From Arthur! (*She takes the letter, opens it and reads*) " Dear Antonia, my uncle is dead. I cannot keep the glorious news from you any longer. Without exaggerating the size of his legacy, I may say that it allows me to be in earnest with a woman. If you love me as I love you, we can very easily come to an understanding. Whatever the other man has been doing for you, I will do — no more and no less. I await your reply." Dear Arthur! Adèle, tell the messenger to kiss the gentleman for me! Send word for him to come! Tell him to come immediately.

ADÈLE

Very well, ma'am. (*Aside*) All the same, I am going to put that little chap's letter on this table, where the missus will see it and open it. (*She goes out*)

ANTONIA

What a surprise! But was n't I just saying that he had something on his mind? He was serious and embarrassed. But why embarrassed? What kept him from telling me what he has written? It does n't hurt a woman's feelings to offer to — his letter is silly — but I don't hold it against him. He does n't know any better. He has n't had practice. (*Going to the table on the left*) Now, then! Now to send the other fellow about his business! When Arthur comes here I want him to find me already free.

Something in strong language! No idle phrases! Just a few stinging words; he 'll understand. (*She writes*) "Idiot! Booby! Spendthrift on yourself and miser with others! Faker! Cuckold!" (*Hesitating*) Should I put that in? Well, it makes it all the stronger. I 'll let it go: "Cuckold!" That 's enough. He does n't deserve anything more. Now the envelope! (*Noticing the letter left by Adèle*) A letter! I 'll read it in a minute. (*Writing the address*) "Mr. Alfred Letourneur. Personal and important." That 's settled. (*Taking the letter left by Adèle*) What does this say? Gracious, it 's poetry!

> Husbands on the watch,
> Lovers that complain,
> Sweethearts yet to come,
> Yesterday's bold swain;
>
> Spite of lying words,
> Spite of ills they do,
> All agree on one thing:
> Women must be true.
>
> Just a passing fancy,
> Just a day's caprice;
> Nothing in the wide world
> Better is than these.
>
> Fair one, hear the voice
> Crying unto you:
> To your love be faithful,
> To your love be true.

That 's pretty poetry, very pretty. The fellow who wrote that understands. What is the writer's name?

Armand Fe — Fe — Felix; no, not Felix — Armand Fecit — Fecit; that's his last name.

ADÈLE (*returning*)

Mr. Arthur, ma'am.

ANTONIA

Show him in. (*Handing Adèle the letter which she has just written*) Adèle, deliver this letter; and don't let anyone disturb us. (*Arthur enters*) Dear Arthur!

ARTHUR

Sweetheart!

ANTONIA

What a hold you have on me!

ARTHUR

What power you have over me! Does my proposal satisfy you?

ANTONIA

I'm delighted with it.

ARTHUR

How good you are to accept it!

ANTONIA

How generous you are to offer it to me!

ARTHUR

Don't thank me, Antonia. Let us love each other with dignity, loyally, serenely; and I shall not regret spending my money.

ANTONIA

Your money, dear — your uncle's money. The first time we go anywhere together it shall be in honor of your uncle, if you like. We shall go to the cemetery, on foot, arm in arm, like a newly married couple, and place a wreath on his grave, with this inscription: (*Interrupting herself*) What was your uncle's name?

ARTHUR

Robinet.

ANTONIA

With this inscription: " To Robinet, from his nephew and niece ! " We 'll have it that way: " And his niece." Can't we?

ARTHUR

All right. We 'll say: " And his niece." And so, Antonia, you do not regret what you are giving up?

ANTONIA

I am thinking only of what I am getting in return.

ARTHUR

Your mind is made up?

ANTONIA

Better than that. The thing is settled.

ARTHUR

I am in my own house, here?

ANTONIA

Yes, dear, you are in your own house.

ARTHUR (*taking her hand and leading her over to the sofa*) Antonia, come here a moment, sit down, and let us talk. Let us talk like two friends, bound together above all else by that affection without which, God knows, the one that takes is the slave of the one that gives. Nevertheless, Antonia dear, you must understand that, when I take on myself such heavy responsibilities, I am assuming that I also acquire certain rights.

ANTONIA (*laying stress on the word*)
Naturally!

ARTHUR

Why do you look at me like that?

ANTONIA

Can't I look at you at all now?

ARTHUR

If I speak to you about the pecuniary sacrifices I have decided to make, it is not because I regret them.

ANTONIA

It will be very soon, dear.

ARTHUR

Don't interrupt me. All I figure on is that they shall serve me better than they did that poor chap whose place I am taking. You acted — scandalously — toward him; there's no other word for it. I found it very funny, I confess. But to-day, when I am taking his place — if another fellow should take mine — ahem! I should n't find it funny at all.

ANTONIA

Stand up! Turn around a little! A little more! What's the matter with your clothes?

ARTHUR

They're all right, are n't they? Genteel and dignified. Don't they become me?

ANTONIA

They make you look thinner. You are not so stout as you used to be.

ARTHUR

Are you going to listen to me?

ANTONIA

I'm listening.

ARTHUR (*sitting down again*)

In our new scheme of things, I am going to draw a hard and fast line between what is beginning and what has gone before. In our new scheme of things —

ANTONIA

Come here. Put your head down here. A white hair! (*She pulls it out*)

ARTHUR

In our new scheme of things —

ANTONIA

White hairs already! You 're going to the dogs!

ARTHUR

In our new scheme of things —

ANTONIA

Say, you know that estate won't come in at all badly, if you are already beginning to have white hairs.

ARTHUR (*losing his patience and folding his arms*)

Antonia!

ANTONIA

I 'm listening, dear; I 'm listening.

ARTHUR

In our new scheme of things I am going to be mighty strict, I can tell you, about your social connections, your diversions, and even your reading. For instance, whenever a spicy novel came out, I used to bring it to you. I should n't let you have it now. We used to go to the Variety Theatre to see some popular comedian four or five times in the same play. No more of that. When I take you anywhere, it will be to a refined, high-class place like the Theatre-Français, or the Opéra-Comique.

ANTONIA

That suits me perfectly. But you, dear — are you clever enough to understand those heavier things?

ARTHUR

What 's that?

ANTONIA

I say, are you clever enough? You are a lively fellow, you know. You like to laugh. You appreciate the kind of show they have at the Palais-Royal — but the higher-class things!

ARTHUR

Shall I go on with what I was saying?

ANTONIA

Go ahead. But it strikes me you are n't quite clever enough.

ARTHUR

I want you to give me a list of all your friends. On this list you will write first the name, then the address, then their business, if they have any. If they have no business — well, I 'll know what that means. Those friends of yours that I know, Antonia, are nice girls, of course, but second-raters.

ANTONIA

Well, what do you expect? I can't associate with the nobility. Why don't you introduce me to your family then?

ARTHUR

Don't exaggerate. I am quite sure that when you are living peacefully, you will make some good acquaintances, meet some proper women — women divorced from their husbands, for instance. There are some.

ANTONIA

Yes, there are a few.

ARTHUR

There are a lot of them — plenty. (*Diffidently*)
Now I am going to take up a more delicate matter
than the rest — about your mother.

ANTONIA

Well, what about my mother?

ARTHUR

You don't see her any more?

ANTONIA

No, dear; we are better off apart.

ARTHUR

Antonia, I want you to go and see your mother and
make up with her. Don't put it off; do it to-morrow.
There is no better society for a woman than that of
her mother.

ANTONIA (*yawning*)

Is that all?

ARTHUR

Yes, that's all — just now, at least. When other
things come to me, I'll speak about them to you.
(*She starts to rise, and he holds her back*) Do you
understand me perfectly, Antonia? In a word, what
is it I want? In the first place, to give our intimacy
the stamp of respectability, which heretofore it
has n't had. Besides, I want to bring into your life
a few notions of discipline, delicacy and morality.

ANTONIA

Oh, he's a windbag; he's a windbag! (*Going over
and sitting down near the table*) Tell me, my dear
— you have spoken of your parents sometimes, but

never about this uncle who left you the money. Was
it long ago that you lost him?

ARTHUR (*embarrassed*)

No, not long. Five or six months.

ANTONIA

Oh, five or six months! Now I do recall that you
were wearing mourning, though you did n't seem
very sad.

ARTHUR

That was for him.

ANTONIA

Then why did n't you tell me the truth?

ARTHUR

Do you want me to tell it to you to-day? I fore-
saw what was coming — that we were going to cast
our lot together. But I had n't then made up my
mind. I was afraid of being stung!

ANTONIA (*aside*)

Being stung!

ARTHUR

You see, I am frank.

ANTONIA

Very frank! Being stung! How much did your
uncle leave you?

ARTHUR (*embarrassed*)

How much did my uncle leave me?

ANTONIA

Yes, your uncle . . . Robinet — what did he leave
you?

ARTHUR

Oh, one hundred and fifty thousand francs.

ANTONIA

Close to two hundred thousand, was n't it?

ARTHUR

Yes, perhaps it will reach two hundred thousand francs.

ANTONIA

Two hundred thousand francs! Fine! That's a lot of money!

ARTHUR

It is a lot of money if it is handled economically. Otherwise it would go quickly enough.

ANTONIA

Ring for Adèle and have her bring my clothes.

ARTHUR

Are you going out?

ANTONIA

We are going out. We're going over to the cemetery. The least you can do is to spend a few hundred francs in flowers and wreaths in honor of a man who has left you a fortune. (*She rises*)

ARTHUR

A few hundred francs! How you talk!

ANTONIA

On the way back from the cemetery, we shall stop in at the dressmaker's. I have a little bill to settle.

ARTHUR

Oh, no, Antonia; no; no bills!

ANTONIA

Am I asking so very much of you? Don't worry, dear. You won't be stung. I am not an extravagant or exacting woman. I have showed you that long ago.

ARTHUR (*going over to her*)

Antonia, this dressmaker's bill — does it amount to much?

ANTONIA

A good deal. (*He retreats*)

ARTHUR (*coming back*)

I say, have n't you some fancy, some whim, that would n't be positively ruinous?

ANTONIA

I don't want a thing.

ARTHUR

Nothing?

ANTONIA

Nothing. Later on, when we have been economical, we shall see.

ARTHUR (*retreating again*)

Very well, later on! Let us wait awhile.

ANTONIA (*going over to him*)

Do you know anything about the Insurance Companies?

ARTHUR

I know about them just as everybody else does.

ANTONIA

It seems that for little or nothing these companies will provide an annuity.

ARTHUR

Oh, no, Antonia; no, no annuities!

ANTONIA

Let 's not talk about it. I want it and I don't want it. I live from day to day. Nevertheless, it would be a comfort for you if you should happen to die. I asked you to ring for Adèle.

ARTHUR (*having rung*)

A word about Adèle. Let her drop this familiar manner she has adopted toward me. She calls me " Mr. Arthur," and sometimes just plain " Arthur."

Have her say " the gentleman "; I am the gentleman now; have her say the " gentleman."

ANTONIA

Very well, dear.

ADÈLE (*entering*)

Did you ring, ma'am?

ANTONIA

Yes; bring me my hat, cloak and gloves.

ADÈLE

Do you want your key, ma'am?

ANTONIA

My key? No, that is n't necessary. (*Adèle goes out at the left*) You have a key to my apartment?

ARTHUR

Yes.

ANTONIA

Give it to me.

ARTHUR

No.

ANTONIA

Don't act like a baby. You are at home now. You can come whenever you please, ring the bell day or night, and not be turned away. You don't need a key.

ARTHUR

That's right, I don't need it. (*He gives her the key*)

ANTONIA (*in a low voice to Adèle, while dressing*)

Look at him, Adèle. Don't you think he is changed?

ADÈLE

Oh, yes, ma'am; he is like another man.

ANTONIA

> That letter I found on my table — where did it come
> from?

ADÈLE

> I was asked to give it to you, ma'am.

ANTONIA

> You can tell Mr. Armand for me that he writes very
> nicely.

ADÈLE

> Do you wish to see him, ma'am? He is in the kitchen.

ANTONIA

> Why did n't you tell me before? I can't see him
> now.

ARTHUR

> What are they whispering about? (*Coming over to
> Antonia*) Antonia, what are you saying to this girl?

ANTONIA

> I am giving her the instructions you spoke about.

ARTHUR

> I hope, Antonia, that you are not putting me in a
> ridiculous light.

ANTONIA (*aside*)

> No, I 'll restrain myself. (*Taking a bill from the
> table drawer*) Here, put this in your pocket. It 's
> my dressmaker's bill. Remind me to ask you for it.

ARTHUR

> Shall we go?

ANTONIA

> I 'm ready. (*They go out by the rear door*)

ADÈLE

> There is something in the wind, that 's certain. It
> looks as though the missus was about to make a
> change. I 'm going to show the apartment to the

little chap. He 'll see the rest some other time.
(*Going to the door on the left and opening it*) Come
in, sir, come in.

ARMAND (*entering, after looking around him*)

Is she coming in?

ADÈLE

No, she has gone out.

ARMAND

Gone out!

ADÈLE

Yes, but perhaps you won't lose anything by waiting. The lady read your letter and it made a good
impression.

ARMAND

I believe you — such a display of imagination! I 'm
bursting with a sonnet.

ADÈLE

How old might you be?

ARMAND

Twenty.

ADÈLE

And don't you do anything but chase after the
ladies?

ARMAND

I 'm in line for a commission.

ADÈLE

Perhaps I did wrong to help you to get acquainted
with the lady. Such a young and lively fellow is
likely to do silly things.

ARMAND

Silly things! I shall never forget the advice of my
aunt, an old dowager who brought me up in a high-
toned way: "At your age, my boy," she used to

say to me, " you pay — with your company." She
says clever things, my aunt does, like all old-
fashioned women.

ADÈLE (*pinching his ear*)

Hush a minute. Somebody is opening the door.
(*Going to the rear door and opening it a little way*)
Look out! It's the missus coming back! Come here
and stay behind me. (*They station themselves at
the rear, on the left*)

ANTONIA (*bursting in and throwing herself on the sofa*)

What a booby! What an idiot! To make a scene
like that, right at my door, just because a friend of
mine speaks to me! (*She takes off her hat and
gloves*)

ADÈLE (*coming forward*)

Of whom are you speaking, ma'am?

ANTONIA

Of whom? How can you ask? Of my gentleman
friend, who is unbearably jealous and violent!
[*Adèle signals to Armand to show himself, and then
goes out.*

ANTONIA (*observing him*)

Who are you? What are you doing here?

ARMAND

Fair one, hear the voice
Crying unto you:
To your love be faithful,
To your love be true.

ANTONIA

Oh, it's you, the writer of that nice poetry I received? I don't mind your sending me poetry, but
your coming here is peculiar, to say the least.

ARMAND

The second time it will be much less so. And it won't seem so at all the third time.

ANTONIA

He has confidence enough in himself! — What do you want, sir?

ARMAND

To please you.

ANTONIA

That's very difficult.

ARMAND

I'll succeed.

ANTONIA

He's conceited enough! — And how do you plan to do it?

ARMAND

By loving you.

ANTONIA

That's the best thing you've said yet. In the first place, are you a good sport?

ARMAND

Dead game.

ANTONIA

Are you . . . loving?

ARMAND

I can guarantee that.

ANTONIA

Are you jealous?

ARMAND

Why should I be jealous? It's for the other man to be jealous. (*She smiles*) May I sit down?

ANTONIA

No, sir; no, you may not sit down. The jealous man may come in any time.

ARMAND

You can hide me. Where is the hiding place here?

ANTONIA

He knows his little lesson! — You say foolish things, young man, but at your age it is permissible.

ARMAND

At *our* age, Antonia!

ANTONIA

So! Now you are calling me Antonia! Behave or I shall send you away.

ARMAND

You are surprised to find such earnestness, or — to use a better word — such impatience, in a lover who seems to you very young, and yet whose passion dates from a meeting long ago.

ANTONIA

A meeting? Tell me about it. (*She sits down*)

ARMAND

Do you remember, about six months ago, going to the Odéon theatre?

ANTONIA

To the Odéon?

ARMAND

Yes; the play was one of Ambigu's. You seemed very much affected by an incident which happened to the heroine, perhaps finding a parallel in your own life. Seeing those beautiful eyes filled with tears, I said to myself: " She is weeping; that 's a good sign. The cold calculation of self-interest has not yet stifled her better self. I am going to make her acquaintance. She will ask me if I am a good sport, if I am loving, but she will not ask me for anything else." Have I deceived myself?

ANTONIA

No, no, you have not deceived yourself, and I am grateful for the good opinion you have of me. But is this story really true? If it be true, we are already old acquaintances.

ARMAND

Oh, Antonia, really you owe me —

ANTONIA

Hush, sir, hush.

ARMAND

It is seven o'clock — a delightful hour, when the day, closing for everybody else, is beginning for the lover. He falls at the feet of his idol and murmurs to her this tender prayer: Come to dinner with me.

ANTONIA (*taking him by the ear*)

Get up.

ARMAND

Come to dinner with me.

ANTONIA

Get up, now. Don't you hear somebody talking in the hall?

ARMAND (*rising*)

I know who it is.

ANTONIA

Well, speak quickly.

ARMAND

'T is *he*, by heavens; the other man. (*She rises and pushes him to the door at the rear, he talking all the while*) The banker, the silk merchant, the wine agent, the oil magnate; he is eternal; he always arrives at the same moment.

ANTONIA (*at the rear door, which she holds half-open*) Arthur! (*Then quickly returning to Armand, whom she drags over to the door on the left*) Go in there, sir, and don't stir.

[*Armand disappears.*

ARTHUR (*entering in an embarrassed way*)
How do you do, Antonia.

ANTONIA
How do you do. Good night!

ARTHUR
You want me to go?

ANTONIA
I 'm not asking you to linger.

ARTHUR
That 's the same thing. Antonia!

ANTONIA
Are n't you going?

ARTHUR
When shall I see you again?

ANTONIA
Some day or other.

ARTHUR
Is it a separation you are looking for?

ANTONIA
A separation! Big words already! No; a separation would n't suit me just now.

ARTHUR
Then let us make up. Don't sulk about a burst of anger for which I was sorry as soon as it happened.

ANTONIA

You need n't try to excuse yourself, it 's of no use. I don't want any explanation. I want you to go away and leave me alone. My mood of sadness and discouragement is upon me.

ARTHUR

Very well, I 'll go. (*Taking a paper from his pocket*) Here, take this bill. I dropped in at your dressmaker's.

ANTONIA (*having looked over the bill carefully*)

In the future you will wait for my permission before settling my tradesmen's bills. Perhaps, now, you 've been learning things from my dressmaker?

ARTHUR

Learning things?

ANTONIA

Yes. Did n't you try to gossip with her about my account?

ARTHUR

About your account? I was too much occupied with the dressmaker's account. I should think, Antonia, that you 'd appreciate —

ANTONIA (*a trifle excitedly*)

Appreciate what? Do you think you are very generous about the payment of this paltry bill? What do I care for one little bill? There are plenty of men who would be glad to pay for me — not one bill, but fifty bills, all my debts.

ARTHUR

She makes me tired, with her debts, her annuity — there is nothing but money talked about here.

ANTONIA

Listen, my dear, and understand me fully. You don't gain anything with me by being jealous and rude, I warn you. I did what you wished me to. For your sake, I sent away a true friend, a real gentleman, a man of the world, who humored all my whims and had the utmost confidence in me. I never deceived him —

ARTHUR

Antonia!

ANTONIA

I *never* deceived him! You had better pattern after him, or the opposite thing will happen to you.

ARTHUR

But the opposite — that's just what I am asking — the opposite. Antonia, you are forgetting —

ANTONIA

I'm forgetting nothing, sir, nothing. I know what you asked of me and what I have promised you. I haven't promised you love. Love is the foundation of everything in the world. I don't set myself up for a saint. My past life is known well enough, God help me, and if you pick a quarrel about a friend who speaks to me, or about a letter I receive, we shall have a row every five minutes.

ARTHUR

She makes me tired! She makes me tired! She isn't talking about one other man now. She's talking about a crowd.

ANTONIA

That's enough! But don't mention it again. Shake hands — and go away.

ARTHUR
> What!

ANTONIA
> You want to stay, my dear?

ARTHUR
> Certainly.

ANTONIA
> Very well, stay. (*She leaves him, and goes to the rear of the room, takes the card table and puts it where it was when the curtain rose*)

ARTHUR (*who has been watching her*)
> Oh, it 's bezique now! (*Changing his tone*) Antonia! (*No answer*) My dear Antonia!

ANTONIA
> I don't hear you, my dear.

ARTHUR
> Just let me say one word.

ANTONIA
> What 's the use? I would n't answer. Sit down and cut the cards.

ARTHUR (*sitting down mechanically*)
> Antonia, I 've done a foolish thing.

ANTONIA
> Which one?

ARTHUR
> We were happier before.

ANTONIA
> Before what?

ARTHUR
> When I was n't the only one.

ANTONIA

It's too late now, my dear. I have done what you
wanted me to. (*To Adèle, who has just come in*)
What is it, Adèle?

ADÈLE

The gentleman is outside, ma'am. He says the letter
you wrote was terrible. He asks you to forgive him,
ma'am.

ANTONIA

You hear that, Arthur? You can change your mind
if you want to. What do you decide?

ARTHUR

Wait! Here's what I decide! Sssh! (*He rises
softly and goes on tiptoes to the door at the left*)

ANTONIA (*running after him*)

Don't go in there! (*She stops him and places him in
such a way that when the door opens he is concealed
behind it; then, opening the door for Armand*) Come
out, sir! Not a word, or I am lost!
[*Armand comes out, crosses the stage, laughing, and
reaches the door on the right.*

ARTHUR (*passing through the door on the left*)

Already!

ANTONIA (*to Adèle*)

Let him come in. (*She sits down at the card table as
Alfred comes in snivelling*) Sit down, my dear. I
have been waiting patiently for you.

CURTAIN